HBase Design Pattern

Design and implement successful patterns to
develop scalable applications with HBase

Mark Kerzner

Sujee Maniyam

[PACKT] open source*
PUBLISHING   community experience distilled

BIRMINGHAM - MUMBAI

HBase Design Patterns

First published: December 2014

Production reference: 1171214

Published by Packt Publishing Ltd.
Livery Place
35 Livery Street
Birmingham B3 2PB, UK.

ISBN 978-1-78398-104-5

www.packtpub.com

Cover image by Asher W (wishkerman@hotmail.com)

Credits

Authors
Mark Kerzner

Sujee Maniyam

Reviewers
Ricky Ho

Raghu Sakleshpur

Sergey Tatarenko

Commissioning Editor
Amarabha Banerjee

Acquisition Editor
Nikhil Karkal

Content Development Editor
Anand Singh

Technical Editors
Tanvi Bhatt

Rikita Poojari

Copy Editors
Dipti Kapadia

Shambhavi Pai

Neha Vyas

Project Coordinator
Akash Poojary

Proofreaders
Simran Bhogal

Ameesha Green

Paul Hindle

Indexer
Monica Ajmera Mehta

Graphics
Abhinash Sahu

Production Coordinator
Conidon Miranda

Cover Work
Conidon Miranda

About the Authors

Mark Kerzner holds degrees in law, math, and computer science. He has been designing software for many years and Hadoop-based systems since 2008. He is a cofounder of Elephant Scale LLC, a big data training and consulting firm, as well as the co-author of the open source book *Hadoop Illuminated*. He has authored other books and patents as well. He knows about 10 languages and is a Mensa member.

> I would like to acknowledge the help of my colleagues, in particular Sujee Maniyam, and last but not least, of my multitalented family.

Sujee Maniyam has been developing software for 15 years. He is a hands-on expert of Hadoop, NoSQL, and cloud technologies. He is a founder and the Principal at Elephant Scale (`http://elephantscale.com/`), where he consults and teaches big data technologies. He has authored a few open source projects and has contributed to the Hadoop project. He is an author of the open source book *Hadoop Illuminated* (`http://hadoopilluminated.com/`).

He is the founder of the Big Data Gurus meetup in San Jose, CA. He has presented at various meetups and conferences.

You can find him on LinkedIn at `http://www.linkedin.com/in/sujeemaniyam` or read more about him at `http://sujee.net`.

> I would like to acknowledge all the kind souls who have helped me along the way. Special thanks go to my co-author, Mark Kerzner, who is also a cofounder and a dear friend and, not the least, thanks goes to my family — my understanding wife and two young kids — who put up with my crazy schedule.

About the Reviewers

Ricky Ho is a data scientist and programmer, providing advisory and development services in big data analytics, machine learning, and distributed system design projects. He has a wide range of technical interests but is especially passionate about the intersection of machine learning and big data. He has served as the Principal Architect of Microsoft advertising, implementing scalable prediction systems to optimize advertising revenue within a large, web scale deployment. Prior to this, he was a researcher at Adobe's lab where he processed web log data for predictive analytics related research. Before that, he was a distinguished architect in PayPal's risk management team, where he developed a fraud detection system using machine learning and anomaly detection algorithms. Ricky holds 10 patents in distributed computing and cloud resource optimization. He is also an active technical blogger and shares what he learns on his blog at `http://horicky.blogspot.com`.

Raghu Sakleshpur is a technologist at heart who works in the field of big data, developing and designing solutions specifically in the Hadoop ecosystem. He started off his career in distributed (clustered) systems and transitioned to developing Enterprise Java application (middleware) space, only to return to his true passion of handling big data in both scaled up and scaled out architectures. He is currently working with Intel in the field of big data and spends a good portion of his time working with customers and partners alike to define optimal architectures for specific big data needs.

I would like to thank and acknowledge the patience of my family for putting up with my weird work hours and a special thanks to Mark Kerzner for providing me with the privilege to review his work.

Sergey Tatarenko is a senior software developer in a major legal e-discovery company in Austin, TX. He received his MSc in Computer Science from Ben-Gurion University of the Negev in Israel and has worked as a software developer since 1999. He started his professional career at Clockwork Solutions, Israel, and worked on a product that was used to build discrete event simulation models. Later, he lead a team of software developers in HyperRoll, but staying farther away from actual software development was not so much fun. In 2008, Sergey agreed to relocate to USA and help his previous employer to finish building their product. In April 2013, he decided to get himself more exposed to big data and started working for a leading legal e-discovery company in Austin, TX. In addition to being a software developer, Sergey is a proud father of three beautiful kids—Ilia, Antony, and Emilia—and a happy husband to his beautiful wife, Ilona. He is also a very active member in the Russian-speaking community of Austin, an enthusiastic builder of Arduino projects at home, and an occasional fisherman.

I would like to thank Mark Kerzner for his wonderful lectures on Hadoop; my dear wife, Ilona, for just being around; and my sweet kids for leaving me some spare time to work on this book. This is my first review and I sincerely hope, my comments will help to make this book better.

www.PacktPub.com

Support files, eBooks, discount offers, and more

For support files and downloads related to your book, please visit www.PacktPub.com.

Did you know that Packt offers eBook versions of every book published, with PDF and ePub files available? You can upgrade to the eBook version at www.PacktPub.com and as a print book customer, you are entitled to a discount on the eBook copy. Get in touch with us at service@packtpub.com for more details.

At www.PacktPub.com, you can also read a collection of free technical articles, sign up for a range of free newsletters and receive exclusive discounts and offers on Packt books and eBooks.

https://www2.packtpub.com/books/subscription/packtlib

Do you need instant solutions to your IT questions? PacktLib is Packt's online digital book library. Here, you can search, access, and read Packt's entire library of books.

Why subscribe?

- Fully searchable across every book published by Packt
- Copy and paste, print, and bookmark content
- On demand and accessible via a web browser

Free access for Packt account holders

If you have an account with Packt at www.PacktPub.com, you can use this to access PacktLib today and view 9 entirely free books. Simply use your login credentials for immediate access.

Table of Contents

Preface

Software plays a paramount role in today's world, and NoSQL databases are an important part of the modern stack. They are found wherever a subsecond response access to vast amounts of information is needed. However, there is a huge gap between the first "Hello World" example in a NoSQL database and creating practical, scalable, and stable applications. The aim of this book is to fill this gap and to give you practical guidelines for building NoSQL software.

The book is specifically formulated in terms of HBase, and there are a few areas of design where HBase might be different from Cassandra or MongoDB, for example, but most of the design patterns discussed here can be transferred to other NoSQL databases. You are expected to invest efforts in learning, which will lead to rewarding skills in the end.

What this book covers

Chapter 1, Starting Out with HBase, covers what HBase is and the various ways in which you can install it on your computer or cluster of computers, with practical advice on the development environment.

Chapter 2, Reading, Writing, and Using SQL, covers the HBase shell and gives the first example of Java code to read and write data in HBase. It also covers using the Phoenix driver for higher-level access, which gives back SQL, justifying the "Not-only-SQL" meaning of NoSQL.

Chapter 3, Using HBase Tables for Single Entities, covers the simplest HBase tables to deal with single entities, such as the table of users. Design patterns in this chapter emphasize on scalability, performance, and planning for special cases, such as restoring forgotten passwords.

Chapter 4, Dealing with Large Files, covers how to store large files in HBase systems. It also covers the alternative ways of storing them and the best practices extracted from solutions for large environments, such as Facebook, Amazon, and Twitter.

Chapter 5, Time Series Data, shows that stock market, human health monitoring, and system monitoring data are all classified as time series data. The design patterns for this organize time-based measurements in groups, resulting in balanced, high-performing HBase tables. Many lessons are learned from OpenTSDB.

Chapter 6, Denormalization Use Cases, discusses one of the most common design patterns for NoSQL denormalization, where the data is duplicated in more than one table, resulting in huge performance benefits. It also shows when to unlearn one's SQL normalization rules and how to apply denormalization wisely.

Chapter 7, Advanced Patterns for Data Modeling, shows you how to implement a many-to-many relationship in HBase that deals with transactions using compound keys.

Chapter 8, Performance Optimization, covers bulk loading for the initial data load into HBase, profiling HBase applications, benchmarking, and load testing.

What you need for this book

All the software used in this book is open source and free. You need Linux and Internet access. The book teaches you how to download and install the rest.

Who this book is for

If you deal with implementing practical big data solutions, involving quick access to massive amounts of data, this is the book for you. Primarily intended for software developers and architects, it can also be used by project managers, investors, and entrepreneurs who plan software implementations.

Conventions

In this book, you will find a number of text styles that distinguish between different kinds of information. Here are some examples of these styles and an explanation of their meaning.

Code words in text, database table names, folder names, filenames, file extensions, pathnames, dummy URLs, user input, and Twitter handles are shown as follows: "The key is what you save when EC2 created the key pair for you, and `<cm-url>` is the URL of the server where you run the Cloudera Manager."

A block of code is set as follows:

```
private void generate(int nUsers, int nEmails) throws IOException {
        SimpleDateFormat dateFormat = new SimpleDateFormat
("yyyy-MM-dd HH:mm:ss");
        new File(Util.ROOT_DIR).mkdirs();
        Charset charset = Charset.forName("US-ASCII");
        if (nEmails < 1) {
            nEmails = 1;
        }
```

Any command-line input or output is written as follows:

```
./sqlline.sh localhost $HBASE_BOOK_HOME/generated/users.txt
```

New terms and **important words** are shown in bold. Words that you see on the screen, for example, in menus or dialog boxes, appear in the text like this: "Also, you can see how **Start Key** and **End Key**, we specified, are showing up."

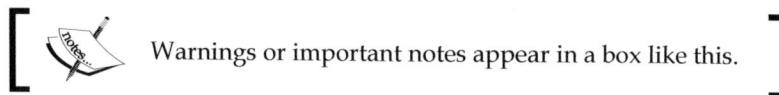

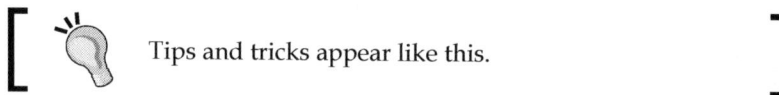

> Warnings or important notes appear in a box like this.

> Tips and tricks appear like this.

Reader feedback

Feedback from our readers is always welcome. Let us know what you think about this book—what you liked or disliked. Reader feedback is important for us as it helps us develop titles that you will really get the most out of.

To send us general feedback, simply e-mail feedback@packtpub.com, and mention the book's title in the subject of your message.

If there is a topic that you have expertise in and you are interested in either writing or contributing to a book, see our author guide at www.packtpub.com/authors.

Customer support

Now that you are the proud owner of a Packt book, we have a number of things to help you to get the most from your purchase.

Downloading the example code

You can download the example code files from your account at `http://www.packtpub.com` for all the Packt Publishing books you have purchased. If you purchased this book elsewhere, you can visit `http://www.packtpub.com/support` and register to have the files e-mailed directly to you.

Errata

Although we have taken every care to ensure the accuracy of our content, mistakes do happen. If you find a mistake in one of our books—maybe a mistake in the text or the code—we would be grateful if you could report this to us. By doing so, you can save other readers from frustration and help us improve subsequent versions of this book. If you find any errata, please report them by visiting `http://www.packtpub.com/submit-errata`, selecting your book, clicking on the **Errata Submission Form** link, and entering the details of your errata. Once your errata are verified, your submission will be accepted and the errata will be uploaded to our website or added to any list of existing errata under the Errata section of that title.

To view the previously submitted errata, go to `https://www.packtpub.com/books/content/support` and enter the name of the book in the search field. The required information will appear under the **Errata** section.

Piracy

Piracy of copyrighted material on the Internet is an ongoing problem across all media. At Packt, we take the protection of our copyright and licenses very seriously. If you come across any illegal copies of our works in any form on the Internet, please provide us with the location address or website name immediately so that we can pursue a remedy.

Please contact us at `copyright@packtpub.com` with a link to the suspected pirated material.

We appreciate your help in protecting our authors and our ability to bring you valuable content.

Questions

If you have a problem with any aspect of this book, you can contact us at `questions@packtpub.com`, and we will do our best to address the problem.

1
Starting Out with HBase

We have already explained the advantages of **HBase** in the preface of this book, where we also dealt with the history and motivation behind HBase. In this chapter, we will make you comfortable with HBase installation. We will teach you how to do the following:

- Create the simplest possible, but functional, HBase environment in a minute
- Build a more realistic one-machine cluster
- Be in full control with clusters of any size

Now it is time for our first cartoon; we will have one for every chapter. This is you, the reader, eager to know the secrets of HBase. With this picture, we understand that learning is a never-ending process.

The simplest way to get HBase up and running takes only a few minutes, and it is so easy that it will almost feel like a cheat, but it's not—you will have a complete HBase development environment.

However, we cannot leave you there. If all you know is building toy clusters, even your most sophisticated HBase design will not command full authority. A pilot needs to know his plane inside out. That is why we will continue with larger and larger cluster installs until you are able to store the planet's data.

Now follow these steps:

1. Download **Kiji** from `http://www.kiji.org/`.
2. Source their environment as per the instructions.
3. Start the cluster.
4. Download **Apache Phoenix** from `http://phoenix.apache.org/download.html`, copy its JAR file into the HBase `lib` directory, and restart the cluster.

Presto! You now have a full HBase development environment that will last you until the end of the book. But remember, to be taken seriously, you need to read till the end and build your clusters.

Installing HBase

The first thing that you need to do when learning to deal with HBase is to install it. Moreover, if you are in any way serious about using HBase, you will want to run it, not on a machine, but on a cluster.

Devops (development and operations) is a modern trend in software development that stresses communication, collaboration, and integration between software developers and information technology professionals. It blurs the distinction between a developer and an administrator.

You will have to live up to this movement in person, by doing what is called **Build Your Own Clusters (BYOC)**. Developers will do well by learning what administrators know, at least to some degree, and the same is true about administrators learning about what developers do.

Why is that? This is primarily because efficiency is the name of the game. The reason you choose a **NoSQL** solution in the first place is for efficiency. Your thoughts around the design will be all around efficiency, that is, the design of the keys, the tables, and the table families. In fact, with NoSQL, you are, for the first time, given the means of *reasoning about the efficiency of your solutions,* to quote from the Google paper on **BigTable**, while doing the logical layout of your data.

So, you will be working on single-node clusters. That's true, but you will always be checking your solutions on larger clusters. Still, we need to start with baby steps.

> **A warning**
>
> I will show you the work in every detail. I often teach courses, and I have noticed how often, users get stuck on minor details. This is because of miscommunication. Once you build your first hundred clusters, it all seems so easy that you forget how hard it was in the beginning, and you tend to skip the details.

Creating a single-node HBase cluster

The easiest way to install a single-node HBase cluster starts by going to the HBase Apache website at `http://hbase.apache.org/`.

Here is what you see there:

The following steps need to be followed:

1. Click on **Downloads**.

2. Choose the mirror that is recommended or try one of your special considerations (if you have a preference), and you will be taken to the following page:

HBase Releases

Please make sure you're downloading from a nearby mirror site, not from www.apache.org.

We suggest downloading the current stable release.

The 0.96.x series supercedes 0.94.x. We are leaving the 'stable' pointer on the latest 0.94.x for now while 0.96 is still 'fresh'.

Name	Last modified	Size	Description
Parent Directory		-	
hbase-0.94.13/	07-Nov-2013 18:40	-	
hbase-0.94.14/	26-Nov-2013 00:39	-	
hbase-0.96.0/	11-Oct-2013 18:39	-	
hbase-0.96.1.1/	19-Dec-2013 14:50	-	
hbase-0.96.1/	16-Dec-2013 13:12	-	
stable/	26-Nov-2013 00:39	-	
to_remove/	07-Apr-2013 16:38	-	

3. Choose the latest distribution, download, and unzip it.

```
mark@mark-dev:~/Downloads$ ls -l
total 3352
-rw-rw-r-- 1 mark mark 3418419 Dec 29 14:30 hbase-0.96.1.1-hadoop1-bin.tar.gz
```

4. Verify the MD5 hash (do not ignore the good software development practices).

```
mark@mark-XPS-8700:~/Desktop$ md5sum hbase-0.98.7-hadoop1-bin.tar.gz
48455b119bd96ca1a44ec4fbbcd63a12  hbase-0.98.7-hadoop1-bin.tar.gz
mark@mark-XPS-8700:~/Desktop$ cat hbase-0.98.7-hadoop1-bin.tar.gz.mds
hbase-0.98.7-hadoop1-bin.tar.gz:    MD5 = 48 45 5B 11 9B D9 6C A1  A4 4E C4 FB
                                    BC D6 3A 12
```

5. Unzip the distribution and change your current directory to the location of the unzipped file as follows:

   ```
   mark@mark-dev:~/Downloads$ gunzip hbase-0.96.1.1-hadoop1-bin.tar.gz
   ```

   ```
   mark@mark-dev:~/Downloads$ tar xf hbase-0.96.1.1-hadoop1-bin.tar
   ```

   ```
   mark@mark-dev:~/Downloads$ cd hbase-0.96.1.1-hadoop1/
   ```

6. Now, start HBase as follows:

   ```
   $ ./bin/start-hbase.sh
   ```

   ```
   starting Master, logging to logs/hbase-user-master-example.org.out
   ```

That's it! You are good to go.

You might get the following message:

```
+======================================================================
|        Error: JAVA_HOME is not set and Java could not be found       |
+----------------------------------------------------------------------+
| Please download the latest Sun JDK from the Sun Java web site        |
|        > http://java.sun.com/javase/downloads/ <                     |
|                                                                      |
| HBase requires Java 1.6 or later.                                    |
| NOTE: This script will find Sun Java whether you install using the   |
|        binary or the RPM based installer.                            |
+======================================================================
```

If this happens to you, set JAVA_HOME in the file conf/hbase-env.sh; for example, as follows:

```
export JAVA_HOME=/usr/lib/jvm/j2sdk1.6-oracle
```

Otherwise, you can set the JAVA_HOME variable in your environment.

Verify your HBase install. Nothing much can go wrong at this stage, so running the HBase shell, as follows, should be enough:

```
mark@mark-dev:~$ hbase shell
13/12/29 14:47:12 WARN conf.Configuration: hadoop.native.lib is
deprecated. Instead, use io.native.lib.available
HBase Shell; enter 'help<RETURN>' for list of supported commands.
Type "exit<RETURN>" to leave the HBase Shell
Version 0.94.6

hbase(main):001:0> status
1 servers, 0 dead, 11.0000 average load

hbase(main):002:0> list
TABLE
EntityGroup
mark_users
mytable
wordcount
4 row(s) in 0.0700 seconds

hbase(main):003:0> exit
mark@mark-dev:~$
```

Except this, you should have no tables at this stage; I just showed you mine.

Now we are ready to go for the real stuff—building a cluster.

Creating a distributed HBase cluster

I am planning to use **Cloudera Manager (CM)** for this, and I will build it on **Amazon Web Services (AWS)** using the **Elastic Compute Cloud (EC2)** web service.

Granted there are other distributions, and there is also your own hardware. However, let me tell you that your own hardware could cost: $26,243.70. This is how much is cost me.

That's just for three machines, which is barely enough for Hadoop work, and with HBase, you might as well double the memory requirements. Although, in the long run, owning your hardware is better than renting, just as the case is with most of the own versus rent scenarios. However, you might prefer to rent Amazon machines, at a fraction of a dollar per hour and for a few minutes of provisioning time.

Now follow these steps:

1. Go to the AWS website at `http://aws.amazon.com/console/`.

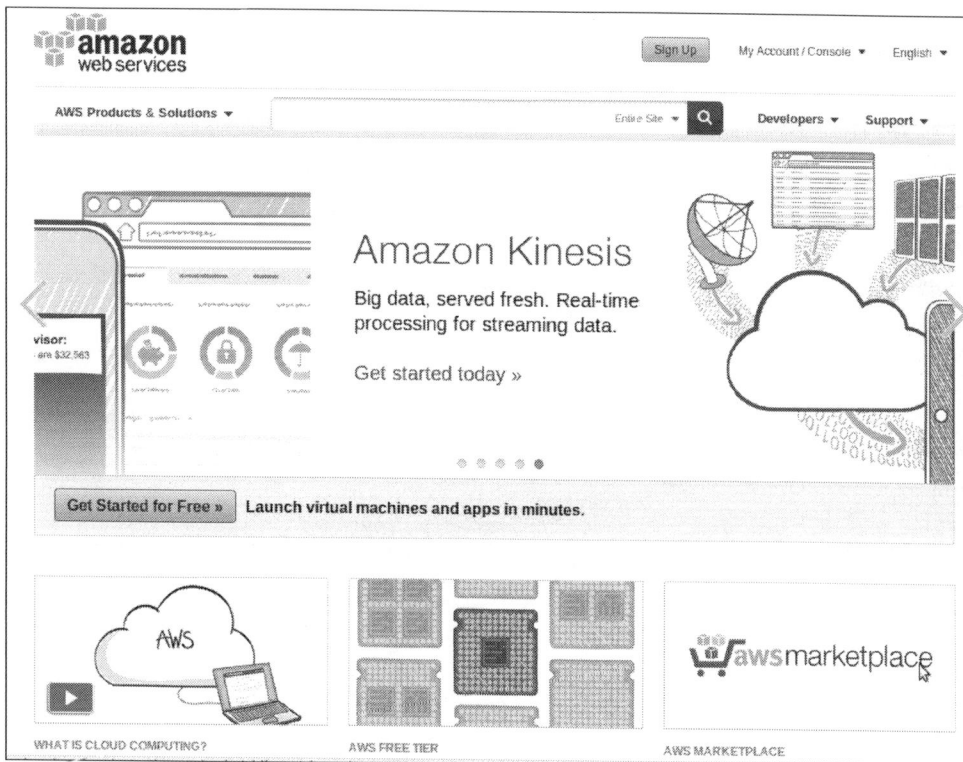

2. Once you are there, log in to the AWS console.

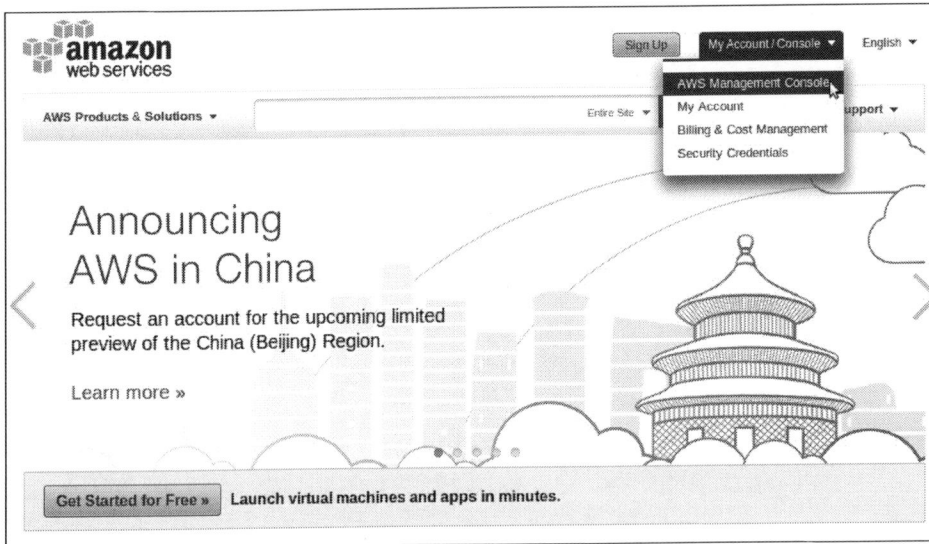

3. Navigate to **EC2**, the Amazon web service.

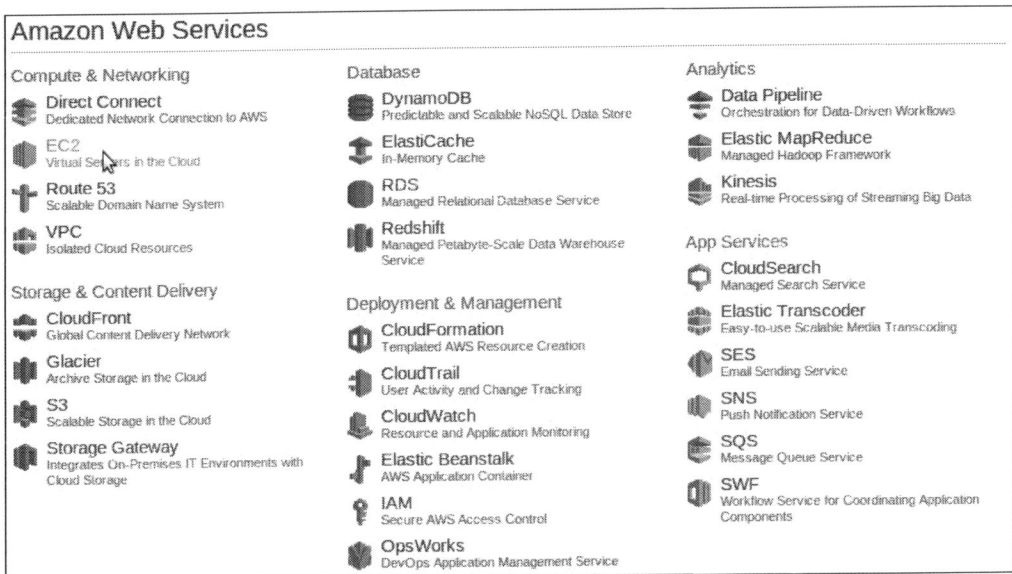

4. Launch your first instance as follows:

5. Choose **Ubuntu Server 12.04.3 LTS** with long-term support.

Choosing Ubuntu Server 12.04.3 LTS with long-term support

Why choose the relatively old version? That is because with Hadoop and HBase, there is no shame in sticking to old versions. There is a good reason for that. The burn-out period for Hadoop is years, running on thousands of machines. So, although you, as a developer, will always prefer the latest and greatest, check yourself. As the wisdom goes, "Who is strong? He who controls his own desires".

There is also another good reason to choose the older version of Ubuntu Server. Most of the Hadoop testing is done on somewhat older versions of the servers. Put yourself in the Hadoop developers' shoes; would you test on a long-term support (seven years) server first, or on the latest and greatest, which promises to put your data in the cloud and to connect you with every social network in the world?

That is why you will have less trouble with the older versions of the OS. I learnt this the hard way.

OK, so now you are convinced and are ready to start your first instance.

Selecting an instance

We start by choosing the **m1.xlarge** file.

1. Choose AMI	2. Choose Instance Type	3. Configure Instance	4. Add Storage	5. Tag Instance	6. Configure Security Group	7. Review

Step 2: Choose an Instance Type

Amazon EC2 provides a wide selection of instance types optimized to fit different use cases. Instances are virtual servers that can run applications. They have varying combinations of CPU, memory, storage, and networking capacity, and give you the flexibility to choose the appropriate mix of resources for your applications. Learn more about instance types and how they can meet your computing needs.

Currently selected: m1.xlarge (8 ECUs, 4 vCPUs, 15 GiB memory, 4 x 420 GiB Storage Capacity)

All instance types

Micro instances
Free tier eligible

General purpose

Memory optimized

Storage optimized

Compute optimized

General purpose

General purpose instances provide a balance of compute, memory, and network resources, and are a good choice for many applications. They are recommended for small and medium databases, data processing tasks that require additional memory, caching fleets, and for running backend servers for SAP, Microsoft SharePoint, and other enterprise applications.

Size	ECUs	vCPUs	Memory (GiB)	Instance Storage (GiB)	EBS-Optimized Available	Network Performance
m1.small	1	1	1.7	1 x 160	-	Low
m1.medium	2	1	3.7	1 x 410	-	Moderate
m1.large	4	2	7.5	2 x 420	Yes	Moderate
m1.xlarge	8	4	15	4 x 420	Yes	High
m3.xlarge	13	4	15	2 x 40 (SSD)	Yes	Moderate
m3.2xlarge	26	8	30	2 x 80 (SSD)	Yes	High

M1 instances are based on Intel Xeon processors.
For M3 instances, each vCPU is a hardware hyperthread from Intel Xeon E5-2670 processors.

Cancel   Previous   Review and Launch   Next: Configure Instance Details

Now, you may wonder how much this is going to cost you. First of all, let me give you a convenient table that summarizes AWS costs. Without it, you would have to browse the Amazon services for quite a while. Follow the link at `http://www.ec2instances.info/`, and here is what you see there. The following table is quite useful:

EC2Instances.info Easy Amazon EC2 Instance Comparison

Region: US East · Cost: Hourly · Search:

Name	Memory	Compute Units	Storage	Architecture	I/O Performance	Max IPs	API Name	Linux cost	Windows cost
Micro	0.60 GB	2 (only for short bursts)	0 GB (EBS only)	32/64-bit	Low	1	t1.micro	$0.02 hourly	$0.02 hourly
M1 Small	1.70 GB	1 (1 core x 1 unit)	160 GB	32/64-bit	Moderate	8	m1.small	$0.06 hourly	$0.09 hourly
M1 Medium	3.75 GB	2 (1 core x 2 units)	410 GB	32/64-bit	Moderate	12	m1.medium	$0.12 hourly	$0.18 hourly
High-CPU Medium	1.70 GB	5 (2 cores x 2.5 units)	350 GB	32/64-bit	Moderate	12	c1.medium	$0.14 hourly	$0.23 hourly
C3 Large	3.75 GB	7 (2 x Intel Xeon E5-2680 v2)	32 GB (2x16 GB SSD)	64-bit	Moderate	1	c3.large	$0.15 hourly	$0.23 hourly
M1 Large	7.50 GB	4 (2 cores x 2 units)	850 GB (2x420 GB)	64-bit	Moderate / 500 Mbps	30	m1.large	$0.24 hourly	$0.36 hourly
C3 Extra Large	7.50 GB	14 (4 x Intel Xeon E5-2680 v2)	80 GB (2x40 GB SSD)	64-bit	High / 1000 Mbps	1	c3.xlarge	$0.30 hourly	$0.47 hourly
High-Memory Extra Large	17.10 GB	6.5 (2 cores x 3.25 units)	420 GB	64-bit	Moderate	60	m2.xlarge	$0.41 hourly	$0.51 hourly
M1 Extra Large	15.00 GB	8 (4 cores x 2 units)	1690 GB (4x420 GB)	64-bit	High / 1000 Mbps	60	m1.xlarge	$0.48 hourly	$0.73 hourly
M3 Extra Large	15.00 GB	13 (4 cores x 3.25 units)	0 GB (EBS only)	64-bit	Moderate / 500 Mbps	60	m3.xlarge	$0.50 hourly	$0.78 hourly
High-CPU Extra Large	7.00 GB	20 (8 cores x 2.5 units)	1690 GB (4x420 GB)	64-bit	High / 1000 Mbps	60	c1.xlarge	$0.58 hourly	$0.90 hourly
C3 Double Extra Large	15.00 GB	28 (8 x Intel Xeon E5-2680 v2)	160 GB (2x80 GB SSD)	64-bit	Very High	1	c3.2xlarge	$0.60 hourly	$0.93 hourly
GPU Double Extra Large	15.00 GB	26 (3.25 x Intel Xeon E5-2670), 1 x NVIDIA GRID GPU (Kepler GK104)	60 GB (1x60 GB SSD)	64-bit	High / 1000 Mbps	1	g2.2xlarge	$0.65 hourly	$0.77 hourly
High-Memory Double Extra Large	34.20 GB	13 (4 cores x 3.25 units)	850 GB	64-bit	Moderate / 500 Mbps	120	m2.2xlarge	$0.82 hourly	$1.02 hourly
I2 Extra Large	30.50 GB	14 (4 x Intel Xeon E5-2670 v2)	800 GB (1x800 GB SSD)	64-bit	Moderate	1	i2.xlarge	$0.85 hourly	$0.97 hourly
M3 Double Extra Large	30.00 GB	26 (8 cores x 3.25 units)	0 GB (EBS only)	64-bit	High / 1000 Mbps	120	m3.2xlarge	$1.00 hourly	$1.58 hourly
C3 Quadruple Extra Large	30.00 GB	55 (16 x Intel Xeon E5-2680 v2)	320 GB (2x160 GB SSD)	64-bit	Very High	1	c3.4xlarge	$1.20 hourly	$1.86 hourly
Cluster Compute Quadruple Extra Large	23.00 GB	33.5 (2 x Intel Xeon X5570)	1690 GB (2x840 GB)	64-bit	Very High	1	cc1.4xlarge	$1.30 hourly	$1.61 hourly
High-Memory Quadruple Extra Large	68.40 GB	26 (8 cores x 3.25 units)	1690 GB (2x840 GB)	64-bit	High / 1000 Mbps	240	m2.4xlarge	$1.64 hourly	$2.04 hourly
I2 Double Extra Large	61.00 GB	27 (8 x Intel Xeon E5-2670 v2)	1,600 GB (2x800 GB SSD)	64-bit	High / 1000 Mbps	1	i2.2xlarge	$1.71 hourly	$1.95 hourly
Cluster GPU Quadruple Extra Large	22.00 GB	33.5 (2 x Intel Xeon X5570), 1 x NVIDIA Tesla M2050 GPU (Fermi GF100)	1690 GB (2x840 GB)	64-bit	Very High	1	cg1.4xlarge	$2.10 hourly	$2.60 hourly
Cluster Compute Eight Extra Large	60.50 GB	88 (2 x Intel Xeon E5-2670)	3370 GB (4x840 GB)	64-bit	Very High	240	cc2.8xlarge	$2.40 hourly	$2.97 hourly
C3 Eight Extra Large	60.00 GB	108 (32 x Intel Xeon E5-2680 v2)	640 GB (2x320 GB SSD)	64-bit	Very High	1	c3.8xlarge	$2.40 hourly	$3.73 hourly
High I/O Quadruple Extra Large	60.50 GB	35 (8 cores + 8 hyperthreads)	2048 GB (2x1024 GB SSD)	64-bit	Very High	1	hi1.4xlarge	$3.10 hourly	$3.58 hourly
I2 Quadruple Extra Large	122.00 GB	53 (16 x Intel Xeon E5-2670 v2)	3,200 GB (4x800 GB SSD)	64-bit	High / 1000 Mbps	1	i2.4xlarge	$3.41 hourly	$3.89 hourly
High Memory Cluster Eight Extra Large	244.00 GB	88 (2 x Intel Xeon E5-2670)	240 GB (2x120 GB SSD)	64-bit	Very High	1	cr1.8xlarge	$3.50 hourly	$3.83 hourly

The AWS costs table

Secondly, in the words of a well-known Houston personality called Mac (or the Mattress Mac)—"I am going to save you money!" (to know more, follow this link at `http://tinyurl.com/kf5vhcg`). Do not click on the **Start the instance** button just yet.

Spot instances

In addition to an on-demand instance, Amazon features what are called **spot instances**. These are machine hours traded on the market, often at one-tenth the price. So, when you are ready to launch your instances, check the **Request spot instances** option, just as I have done in the following screenshot:

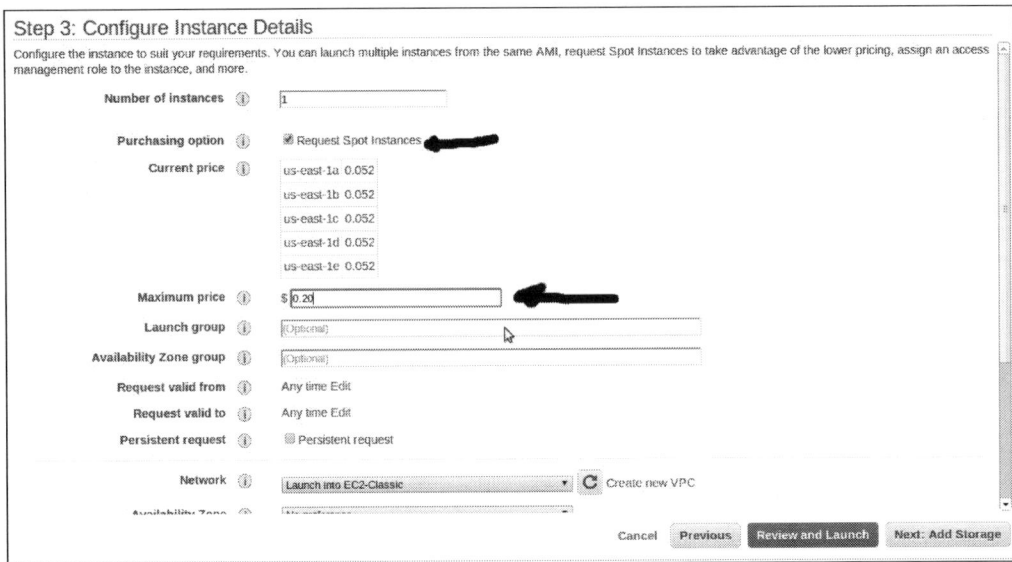

Here are my savings—the `m1.xlarge` instance costs 48 cents an hour when purchased on demand, but its current market price is about 5 cents, about 10 times cheaper. I am setting the maximum offered price at 20 cents, and that means I will be paying the fluctuating market price, starting from 5 cents and possibly up, but not more than 20 cents per hour.

I do not delude myself; I know that the big fish (that is, the big EC2-based companies) are hunting for those savings, and they apply sophisticated trading techniques, which sometimes result in strange pricing, exceeding the on-demand pricing. Be careful with the maximum limit you set. But for our limited purposes of practicing cluster construction, we should swim under the belly of the big fish and be just fine.

Adding storage

The next step is selecting the storage. The Ubuntu image comes with 8 GB of root drive, and that is too little for anything; choose 30 GB for now. Remember that each 1 GB costs 5 cents per month at current prices, so for hours, and even days, that is negligible.

By now, you might be asking yourself, where does Mark know all this from? I will give you the two references now, and I will also repeat them at the end of the chapter (for the benefit of those who like to peek at the end). As I have already told you, I run Hadoop/HBase training, and our labs are all open source. Please have a look at `https://github.com/hadoop-illuminated/HI-labs` for more details. More specifically, in the admin labs, in the **Managers** section (and that means Hadoop, not human managers), you will find the instructions in brief (`https://github.com/hadoop-illuminated/HI-labs/tree/master/hadoop-admin/managers/cloudera-cm`). In turn, it refers to the Cloudera blog post found at `http://blog.cloudera.com/blog/2013/03/how-to-create-a-cdh-cluster-on-amazon-ec2-via-cloudera-manager/`. However, none of these instructions are as complete as this chapter, so save them for future use.

Security groups

Now it is time to set up a security group. Here is my **hadoop** security group. Please note that all servers within this group can communicate with each other on every port. For the outside ports, I have opened those that are required by Cloudera Manager, and by the Hadoop UI for HDFS and MapReduce. Here is me selecting this group for Cloudera Manager I will be using to install the rest of the cluster:

This is my **hadoop** security group:

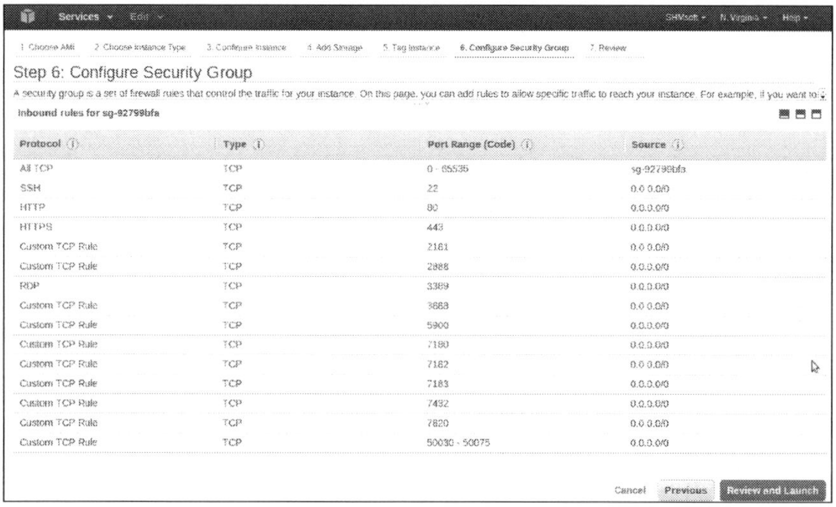

Step 6: Configure Security Group

A security group is a set of firewall rules that control the traffic for your instance. On this page, you can add rules to allow specific traffic to reach your instance. For example, if you want to...

Inbound rules for sg-92799bfa

Protocol ⓘ	Type ⓘ	Port Range (Code) ⓘ	Source ⓘ
All TCP	TCP	0 - 65535	sg-92799bfa
SSH	TCP	22	0.0.0.0/0
HTTP	TCP	80	0.0.0.0/0
HTTPS	TCP	443	0.0.0.0/0
Custom TCP Rule	TCP	2181	0.0.0.0/0
Custom TCP Rule	TCP	2888	0.0.0.0/0
RDP	TCP	3389	0.0.0.0/0
Custom TCP Rule	TCP	3888	0.0.0.0/0
Custom TCP Rule	TCP	5900	0.0.0.0/0
Custom TCP Rule	TCP	7180	0.0.0.0/0
Custom TCP Rule	TCP	7182	0.0.0.0/0
Custom TCP Rule	TCP	7183	0.0.0.0/0
Custom TCP Rule	TCP	7432	0.0.0.0/0
Custom TCP Rule	TCP	7820	0.0.0.0/0
Custom TCP Rule	TCP	50030 - 50075	0.0.0.0/0

> Don't let Cloudera Manager create a group for you — it is better to create it yourself and keep using it.

Starting the instance

Now, we give a final touch as shown in the following screenshot:

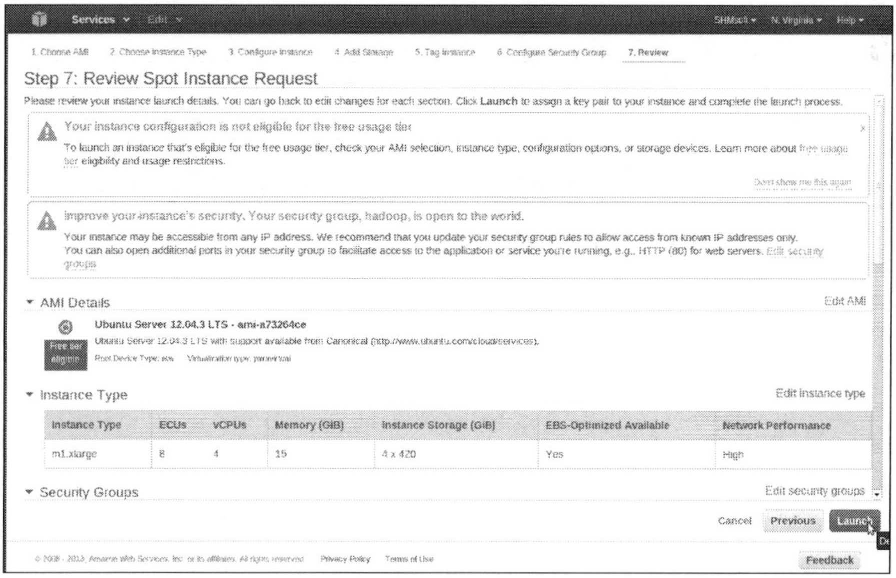

Launching the instance

Choose the key. Again, don't let CM create the key for you. Ask Amazon, and store the key in a secure place.

Hold on, we are almost done. Now, let's start 10 more instances that will be used for cluster construction. There are two reasons why I start them myself rather than asking CM to start them for me. Firstly, it results in saving money. I will start spot instances, whereas CM can only start on-demand ones. Secondly, it has better control. If something does not work, I can see it much better than CM can.

You are familiar by now with most of the steps. Except that this time, I am starting 10 instances at once, saving a lot of money in the process.

These 10 instances will be the workhorses of the cluster, so I will give them enough root space, that is, 100 GB. The CM is smart enough to get the ephemeral storage (about 5 TB) and make it a part of the HDFS. The result will approximately be a 5-TB cluster for one dollar per hour. Here are all of these pending requests:

	Request ID	Max Price	AMI ID	Instance	Type	State	Status
☐	sir-55dc8234	$0.200	ami-a73264ce	📦 i-a078f880	m1.xlarge	⬤ active	fulfilled
☐	sir-0a470634	$0.200	ami-a73264ce		m1.xlarge	⬤ open	pending-evaluation
☐	sir-123fe434	$0.200	ami-a73264ce		m1.xlarge	⬤ open	pending-evaluation
☐	sir-24183a34	$0.200	ami-a73264ce		m1.xlarge	⬤ open	pending-evaluation
☐	sir-2ac23834	$0.200	ami-a73264ce		m1.xlarge	⬤ open	pending-evaluation
☐	sir-2ae93634	$0.200	ami-a73264ce		m1.xlarge	⬤ open	pending-evaluation
☐	sir-4dccc434	$0.200	ami-a73264ce		m1.xlarge	⬤ open	pending-evaluation
☐	sir-77727a34	$0.200	ami-a73264ce		m1.xlarge	⬤ open	pending-evaluation
☐	sir-92b63634	$0.200	ami-a73264ce		m1.xlarge	⬤ open	pending-evaluation
☐	sir-cf147834	$0.200	ami-a73264ce		m1.xlarge	⬤ open	pending-evaluation
☐	sir-d65b0e34	$0.200	ami-a73264ce		m1.xlarge	⬤ open	pending-evaluation

A few minutes later, here they all are again, with spot requests fulfilled and servers running.

	Name	Instance ID	Instance Type	Availability Zone	Instance State	Status Checks	Alarm Status	Public DNS
	HBase cluster	i-a325a5b3	m1.xlarge	us-east-1e	⬤ running	✓ 2/2 checks passed	None	ec2-54-196-60-157.compute-1.amazonaws.com
	HBase cluster - CM	i-a078f880	m1.xlarge	us-east-1e	⬤ running	✓ 2/2 checks passed	None	ec2-50-17-135-161.amazonaws.com
	HBase cluster	i-4f1b9b6f	m1.xlarge	us-east-1e	⬤ running	✓ 2/2 checks passed	None	ec2-54-205-27-58.compute-1.amazonaws.com
	HBase cluster	i-eb27a7cb	m1.xlarge	us-east-1e	⬤ running	✓ 2/2 checks passed	None	ec2-54-243-4-218.compute-1.amazonaws.com
	HBase cluster	i-ee27a7ce	m1.xlarge	us-east-1e	⬤ running	✓ 2/2 checks passed	None	ec2-54-196-65-31.compute-1.amazonaws.com
	HBase cluster	i-a827a7c8	m1.xlarge	us-east-1e	⬤ running	✓ 2/2 checks passed	None	ec2-23-20-114-89.compute-1.amazonaws.com
	HBase cluster	i-e927a7c9	m1.xlarge	us-east-1e	⬤ running	✓ 2/2 checks passed	None	ec2-54-204-62-13.compute-1.amazonaws.com
	HBase cluster	i-ba22a29a	m1.xlarge	us-east-1e	⬤ running	✓ 2/2 checks passed	None	ec2-184-72-198-189.compute-1.amazonaws.com
	HBase cluster	i-b722a297	m1.xlarge	us-east-1e	⬤ running	✓ 2/2 checks passed	None	ec2-54-243-25-98.compute-1.amazonaws.com
	HBase cluster	i-b422a294	m1.xlarge	us-east-1e	⬤ running	✓ 2/2 checks passed	None	ec2-54-196-164-128.compute-1.amazonaws.com
	HBase cluster	i-b522a295	m1.xlarge	us-east-1e	⬤ running	✓ 2/2 checks passed	None	ec2-54-204-150-163.compute-1.amazonaws.com

Fulfilled requests and running servers

Now comes your part — building the cluster. Remember, so far Amazon has been working for you, you just provided the right foundation.

Now, log in to the CM machine as follows:

```
ssh -i .ssh/<your-key-here.pem> ubuntu@<cm-url>
```

The key is what you saved when EC2 created the key pair for you, and `<cm-url>` is the URL of the server where you run the Cloudera Manager. Note that I carefully assign the servers their names. Soon, you will have many servers running, and if you don't mark them, it will get confusing. Now, start the install using the following command:

```
wget http://archive.cloudera.com/cm5/installer/latest/cloudera-
manager-installer.bin

chmod +x cloudera-manager-installer.bin

sudo ./cloudera-manager-installer.bin
```

CM will take you through a series of screenshots, and you will have to accept a couple of licenses. There are no choices and no gotchas here, so I am showing only one intermediate screen:

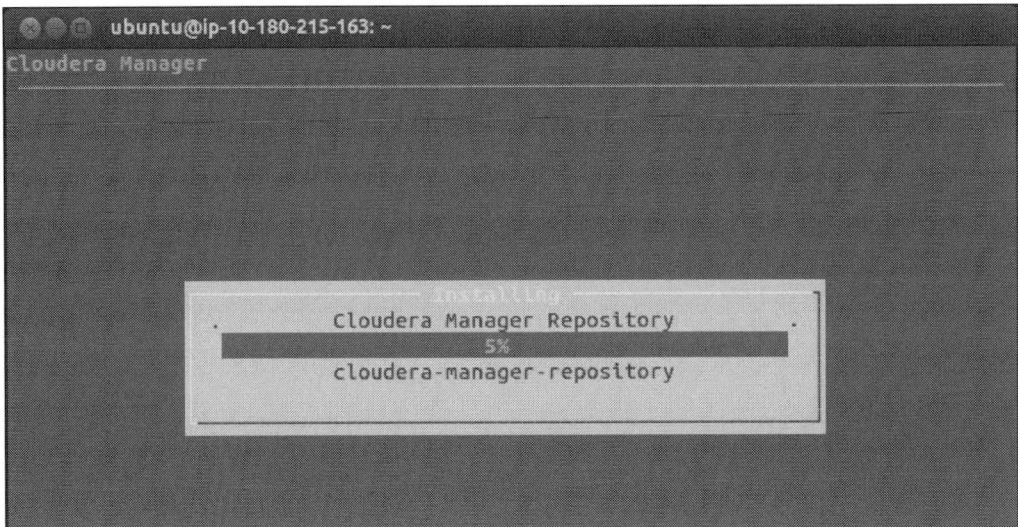

After this is done, give it a minute to start the web server. Then go to `<cm-url>:7180`. In my case, this looks as follows:

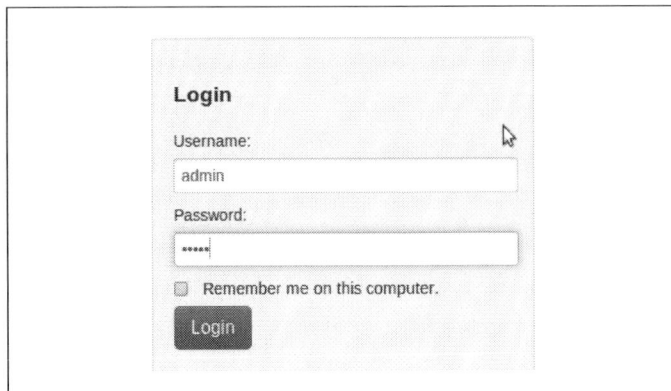

Log in with both **Username** and **Password** as admin. Accept the free license and continue to the **Hosts** screen. Now is probably the most important selection. Get the private DNS for every host in the cluster and put it into the **Check Hosts** window.

Specify hosts for your CDH cluster installation.

Cloudera recommends including Cloudera Manager server's host because it is often used for the Cloudera Management Service, and because this will enable health monitoring for that host.

Hint: Search for hostnames and/or IP addresses using patterns ⌗.

```
ip-10-180-215-132.ec2.internal
ip-10-180-209-232.ec2.internal
ip-10-180-207-41.ec2.internal
ip-10-180-202-34.ec2.internal
```

SSH Port: 22   🔍 Search

◄ Back   ►► Continue

One last note, and then I will let you kids go play with your cluster and fly solo. Why is it so important to choose the internal IP, also called the private DNS? Firstly, because you won't be charged for every request. Normally, you get charged for every request and transfer, but for internal transfers, this charge is zero, that is free — nada! Secondly, recall that in our security group, all servers are allowed to communicate with all other servers on all ports. So you won't have any problems setting up your clusters, regardless of which ports the Hadoop services decide to communicate on. If you don't do that, the install will fail on the next step. However, if everything is correct, you will get this happy screen:

cloudera manager   Support ⌄   👤 admin ⌄

Specify hosts for your CDH cluster installation.

Cloudera recommends including Cloudera Manager server's host because it is often used for the Cloudera Management Service, and because this will enable health monitoring for that host.

Hint: Search for hostnames and/or IP addresses using patterns ⌗.

11 hosts scanned, 11 running SSH.   🔍 New Search

☑ Expanded Query	Hostname (FQDN)	IP Address	Currently Managed	Result
☑ ip-10-180-188-14.ec2.internal	ip-10-180-188-14.ec2.internal	10.180.188.14	No	✓ Host ready: 2,629 ms response time.
☑ ip-10-180-199-186.ec2.internal	ip-10-180-199-186.ec2.internal	10.180.199.186	No	✓ Host ready: 2,842 ms response time.
☑ ip-10-180-202-34.ec2.internal	ip-10-180-202-34.ec2.internal	10.180.202.34	No	✓ Host ready: 2,665 ms response time.
☑ ip-10-180-207-41.ec2.internal	ip-10-180-207-41.ec2.internal	10.180.207.41	No	✓ Host ready: 2,364 ms response time.
☑ ip-10-180-209-232.ec2.internal	ip-10-180-209-232.ec2.internal	10.180.209.232	No	✓ Host ready: 2,523 ms response time.
☑ ip-10-180-210-220.ec2.internal	ip-10-180-210-220.ec2.internal	10.180.210.220	No	✓ Host ready: 2,205 ms response time.
☑ ip-10-180-215-132.ec2.internal	ip-10-180-215-132.ec2.internal	10.180.215.132	No	✓ Host ready: 3,007 ms response time.
☑ ip-10-180-215-163.ec2.internal	ip-10-180-215-163.ec2.internal	10.180.215.163	No	✓ Host ready: 0 ms response time.
☑ ip-10-180-216-101.ec2.internal	ip-10-180-216-101.ec2.internal	10.180.216.101	No	✓ Host ready: 513 ms response time.
☑ ip-10-180-220-67.ec2.internal	ip-10-180-220-67.ec2.internal	10.180.220.67	No	✓ Host ready: 2,049 ms response time.
☑ ip-10-180-223-114.ec2.internal	ip-10-180-223-114.ec2.internal	10.180.223.114	No	✓ Host ready: 1,893 ms response time.

◄ Back   ►► Continue

Give it the right username (in my case, it is ubuntu) and the right key on the next screen. I can rely on you to do it right, as these are the same username and key that you used to log into the Cloudera Manager server. If you could do that, you will be able to do this as well.

Don't leave your monitor unattended, so keep clicking at the right times. If you don't, the CM session will time out and you won't be able to restart the install. All the work will be lost; you will have to shut all the servers down and restart them. You've been warned, so get your coffee ready before you start!

It is not uncommon for some servers to fail to start. This is normal in clusters and in a networked environment. CM will drop the servers that fail to start for any reason and continue with what it has.

As a wise man said, "Who is rich? One who is happy with what he has."

On one of the next screens, do not forget to request HBase as part of the real-time delivery. There is no deep meaning to this, just marketing, as it is you who will provide the actual real-time delivery with HBase and your code.

Finally, enjoy your new cluster, kick the tires, look around, try to look at every service that is installed, analyze each individual host, and so on. You can always come back home by clicking on the **Home** or **Cloudera** button at the top-left of the screen.

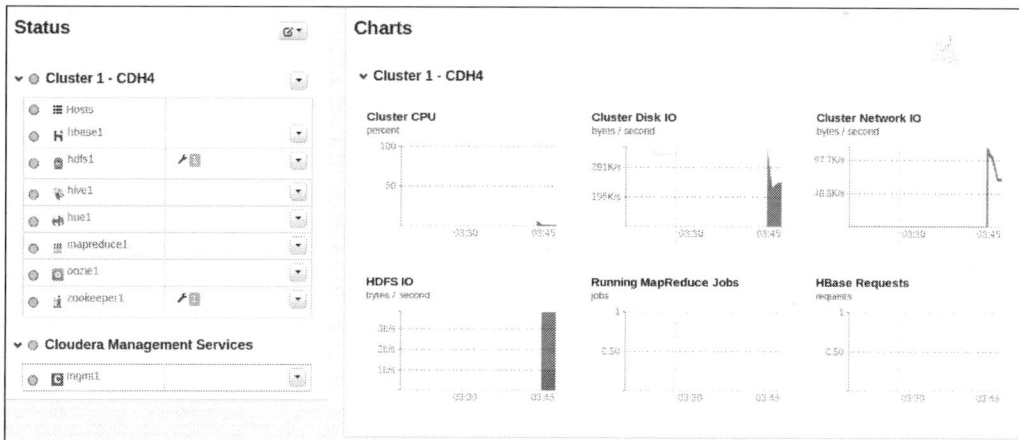

Log in to the cluster. Any of the 11 servers, including CM, is good for that, because the Gateway service is installed on each one of them. In my case, the login command looks as follows:

```
mark@mark-dev:~$ ssh -i .ssh/shmsoft-hadoop.pem ubuntu@ec2-50-17-135-
161.compute-1.amazonaws.com
```

Once there, I can look around HDFS as follows:

```
ubuntu@ip-10-180-215-163:~$ hdfs dfs -ls /

Found 3 items

drwxr-xr-x    - hbase hbase            0 2014-12-30 03:41 /hbase

drwxrwxrwt    - hdfs  supergroup       0 2014-12-30 03:45 /tmp

drwxr-xr-x    - hdfs  supergroup       0 2014-12-30 03:43 /user
```

However, if you try to create your home directory, it won't work:

```
hdfs dfs -mkdir /user/ubuntu

mkdir: Permission denied: user=ubuntu, access=WRITE,
inode=""/user"":hdfs:supergroup:drwxr-xr-x
```

To fix this, you need to do the following (as described at https://github. com/hadoop-illuminated/HI-labs/tree/master/hadoop-admin/managers/ cloudera-cm):

```
ubuntu@ip-10-180-215-163:~$ sudo -u hdfs   hdfs dfs -mkdir   /user/ubuntu

ubuntu@ip-10-180-215-163:~$ sudo -u hdfs  hdfs dfs -chown ubuntu /user/
ubuntu

ubuntu@ip-10-180-215-163:~$ hdfs dfs -mkdir  /user/ubuntu/mark
```

Now you have your home, and in fact, your user directory (mark in my case, so that I can see it):

```
ubuntu@ip-10-180-215-163:~$ hdfs dfs -ls

Found 1 items

drwxr-xr-x    - ubuntu supergroup       0 2014-12-30 04:03 mark
```

Moreover, I can even put files there. For example, I can put my install file in mark/, as follows:

```
hdfs dfs -put cloudera-manager-installer.bin mark/
```

And, lo and behold, I can see that file:

```
hdfs dfs -ls mark

Found 1 items
```

```
-rw-r--r--   3 ubuntu supergroup      501703 2014-12-30 04:04
mark/cloudera-manager-installer.bin
```

Now, two last tricks of the trade. The first is to view the HDFS UI, and the second is to open it in the browser or on the command line:

```
w3m http://ec2-54-205-27-58.compute-1.amazonaws.com:50070
```

If you use the internal IP (which you can find on the AWS console), as follows, then you will not be blocked by the firewall and you will be able to browse at any level:

```
w3m http://10.180.188.14:50070
```

If you want to see the HBase, it is found here:

```
w3m http://10.180.188.14:60010
```

If you have any questions, use the Hadoop illuminated forum found at `http://hadoopilluminated.com/` to ask the authors or your peers.

You will also have many choices of Hadoop distribution and run environments. We have summarized them in the following cartoon:

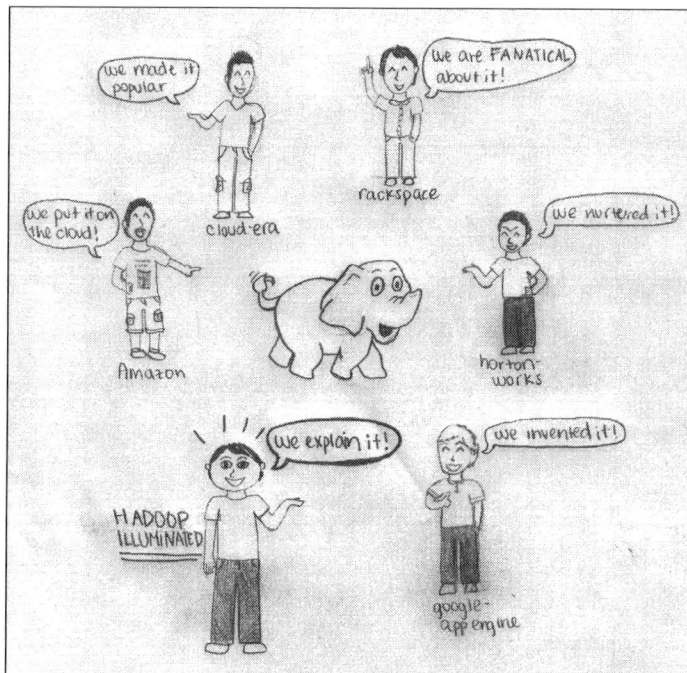

Summary

In this chapter, I convinced you that you will be able to build your own HBase clusters, and then spent a large part of the chapter walking you through this process. Please follow the steps precisely! Many hints that are found here are very important, and without them, the cluster will not work.

Once you are at ease with the basic construction, you will be able to strike on your own, change the ways in which you build those clusters, and eventually come up with something new and unexpected.

Please keep in mind that we used the Cloudera Hadoop distribution as a basis for all the instructions. You are not limited to this; you have a choice. The **Apache BigTop** project is your independent alternative (`http://bigtop.apache.org/`). **HortonWorks** and **MapR** also offer distributions with their managers. All of them provide the same excellent Hadoop distribution. In this book, I wanted to give you a clear set of instructions that worked for me.

For the comparison of different Hadoop distributions, please refer to *Chapter 11, Distributions,* of our open source book *Hadoop Illuminated* (`http://hadoopilluminated.com/hadoop_illuminated/Distributions.html`). If you are interested in the precise installation instructions for other distributions, watch out for our Hadoop illuminated labs at `https://github.com/hadoop-illuminated/HI-labs`. Eventually, all the distributions will be described there, in the admin labs.

Note that there are exactly 33 pictures in this chapter. This, of course, is no coincidence.

Recall the poem by Omar Khayyám, which tells you that there are no coincidences in this world:

> *"The Moving Finger writes; and, having writ,*
>
> *Moves on: nor all thy Piety nor Wit*
>
> *Shall lure it back to cancel half a Line,*
>
> *Nor all thy Tears wash out a Word of it."*

One can argue whether tears can or cannot erase our mistakes, but in this world of clusters, we can always try by repeating the steps again and again.

In the next chapter, we will discuss using Java code to read from and write to HBase. We will also see how we can control HBase with the help of the HBase shell. The most important thing we will learn is to operate through SQL statements, in a manner familiar to all SQL database users.

2
Reading, Writing, and Using SQL

In the first chapter, we learned how to prepare a playground for ourselves. Now, we are ready to use the HBase installation to store and retrieve data and run our code examples.

In this chapter, we will learn about the following topics:

- Reading data from HBase using Java
- Writing data to HBase using Java
- How to forget about all these complexities and go back to using SQL

Originally, NoSQL was *No SQL*, as you had to know Java and you could not use SQL. However, later the developers learned to differentiate that just because you don't have the ACID-stringent requirements usually associated with SQL, it does not mean that you cannot have the convenience and know-how of the SQL idiom. Thus, there appeared multiple NoSQL databases (which by now meant *Not Only SQL*) that could understand the familiar SQL language. **Cassandra** has had **Cassandra Query Language** (CQL) for quite a while, and now, HBase also has a very smart implementation of SQL — project Phoenix. This is what we will introduce you to in this chapter.

Inspecting the cluster

We will now investigate the Hadoop cluster with HBase.

> Never forget to use spot instances, which can be up to 10 times cheaper.

If you build your Hadoop cluster using **Cloudera Manager**, you will see a screen similar to the one we have next. (We are showing Hadoop 1 and the CDH4 distribution, and you will most likely be dealing with the next version, Hadoop 2, but for our exploration of HBase, it will make little difference.)

The screenshot we just saw (in the previous chapter) shows multiple Hadoop services running; HBase being one of them. HBase in turn depends on HDFS and ZooKeeper. Here, all should be in good working order.

To go to HBase, click on the **hbase1** service on the left-hand side of the following screenshot, and you will be taken to the screen dedicated to HBase, as shown here:

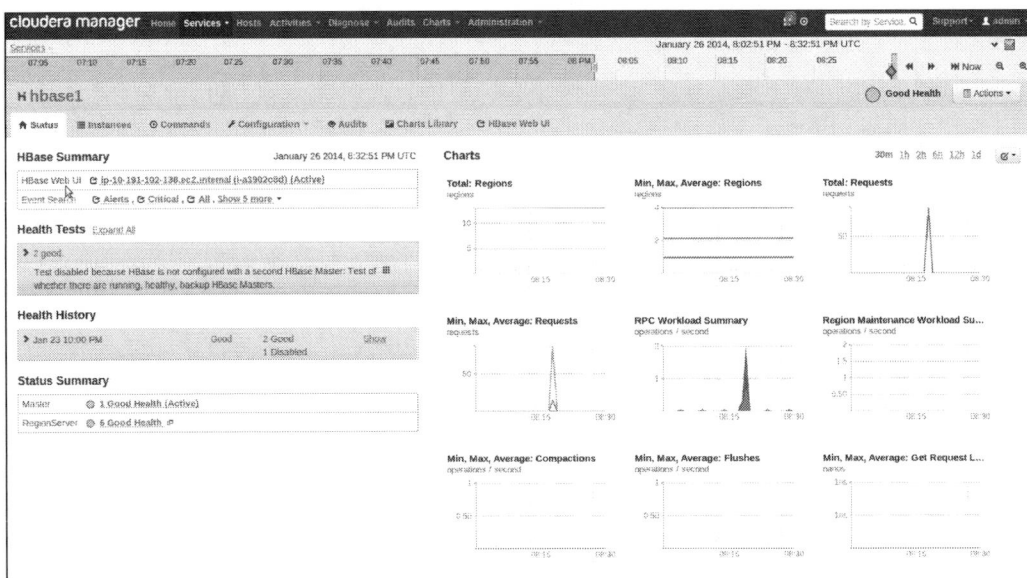

The HBase screen

The screenshot we just saw shows specific HBase metrics. It is useful to verify the health of the database and to check for bottlenecks in performance.

Go ahead and click on **HBase Web UI**, and you will be taken to the HBase provided UI, as shown in the next screenshot:

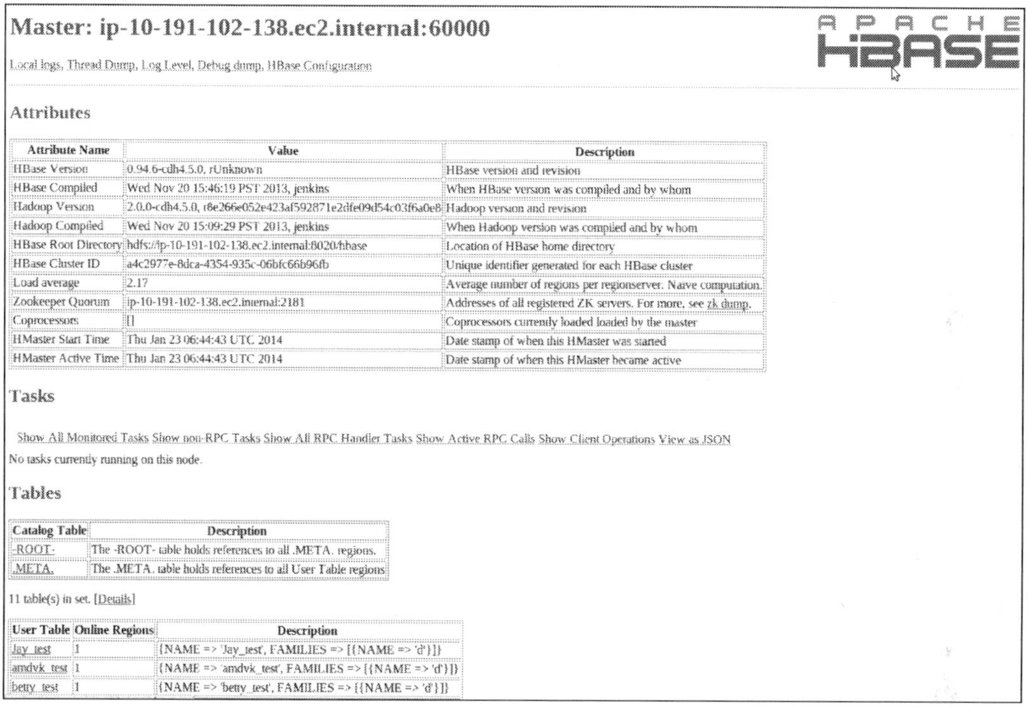

The following screenshot shows you HBase information such as build, time up, Zookeeper, and so on. While the previous two screenshots were part of Cloudera Manager (other managers would provide you with similar monitoring functionality), the following screenshot comes as part of HBase. It also shows you the tables currently present in HBase.

If you are experimenting with HBase using a local installation, this will look pretty much the same, but will feature only one **RegionServer**, as follows:

Master: mark-7:60000

Local logs, Thread Dump, Log Level, Debug dump, HBase Configuration

Attributes

Attribute Name	Value	Description
HBase Version	0.94.6-cdh4.5.0, rUnknown	HBase version and revision
HBase Compiled	Wed Nov 20 15:48:11 PST 2013, jenkins	When HBase version was compiled and by whom
Hadoop Version	2.0.0-cdh4.5.0, r8e266e052e423af592871e2dfe09d54c03f6a0e8	Hadoop version and revision
Hadoop Compiled	Wed Nov 20 15:10:35 PST 2013, jenkins	When Hadoop version was compiled and by whom
HBase Root Directory	hdfs://mark-7:8020/hbase	Location of HBase home directory
HBase Cluster ID	8c7e0bc7-e22f-4572-95e5-8b2aa04826b3	Unique identifier generated for each HBase cluster
Load average	13.00	Average number of regions per regionserver. Naïve computation.
Zookeeper Quorum	mark-7:2181	Addresses of all registered ZK servers. For more, see zk dump.
Coprocessors	[]	Coprocessors currently loaded loaded by the master
HMaster Start Time	Sat Jan 25 22:36:53 CST 2014	Date stamp of when this HMaster was started
HMaster Active Time	Sat Jan 25 22:36:53 CST 2014	Date stamp of when this HMaster became active

Tasks

Show All Monitored Tasks Show non-RPC Tasks Show All RPC Handler Tasks Show Active RPC Calls Show Client Operations View as JSON

No tasks currently running on this node.

Tables

Catalog Table	Description
-ROOT-	The -ROOT- table holds references to all .META. regions.
.META.	The .META. table holds references to all User Table regions.

7 table(s) in set. [Details]

User Table	Online Regions	Description
kiji.default.meta	1	{NAME => 'kiji.default.meta', FAMILIES => [{NAME => 'layout', VERSIONS => '2147483647'}, {NAME => 'meta', VERSIONS => '2147483647'}]}
kiji.default.schema_hash	1	{NAME => 'kiji.default.schema_hash', FAMILIES => [{NAME => 'schema', VERSIONS => '2147483647'}]}
kiji.default.schema_id	1	{NAME => 'kiji.default.schema_id', FAMILIES => [{NAME => 'schema', VERSIONS => '2147483647'}]}
kiji.default.system	1	{NAME => 'kiji.default.system', FAMILIES => [{NAME => 'value', VERSIONS => '1'}]}

This screenshot shows you a sample HBase configuration for a single-node install. Please note that you can access it on the `localhost:60010` URL; the computer used in this case is called `mark-7`.

The environment described here should work for you. If not, you need to spend some time preparing and fixing it. Please visit `http://hbasedesignpatterns.com/` for discussion and help.

HBase tables, families, and cells

Let's briefly review the basic HBase data structure. HBase has tables that are similar to SQL tables. It has families that show you ways to organize columns together. There is nothing very special about these, except that columns belonging to one family are guaranteed to be stored in physical proximity of each other, so that it makes sense for you to group into families columns that are usually accessed together. This, as the authors of BigTable (the model for HBase) state, allows the developer to reason about the efficiency of data access.

Now, for the power and special features of HBase, all the data stored is based on the **row key**. This is a unique key that identifies the logical storage of all the columns in a row. HBase stores its data sorted by the row key. This assures fast read access.

Based on the row key, HBase stores the row. Rows consist of columns. Columns are created dynamically by storing [column_name] and [column_value]. Thus, you don't need to define a column name before using it, and not all columns have to be present in every row. This is why HBase is called a **column-oriented** store. In addition, each cell is stored with a time stamp.

This can be summarized concisely by stating that HBase is a distributed, giant hash table, with sorted keys for fast access. This might not reflect all the power of HBase, but it serves as a good first approximation. For more details, you can refer to the book *HBase Essentials* by Packt Publishing.

All this becomes very clear when you use the HBase shell, so let's proceed to it right away.

The HBase shell

The HBase shell is great because it gives you the first handle on HBase. It allows you to create, modify, and delete tables; put and get values; and run scans. It is only a simple interface and not really programmable (for that you still need Java, but it is a start.)

Now, it is time to start creating the HBase shell. Type in the following command, which you can type on the Linux command prompt:

```
hbase shell
```

On clicking *Enter*, you will see the following output:

```
HBase Shell; enter 'help<RETURN>' for list of supported commands.
Type "exit<RETURN>" to leave the HBase Shell
Version 0.94.6-cdh4.5.0, rUnknown, Wed Nov 20 15:48:11 PST 2013
hbase(main):001:0>
```

Once you see this output, you will know that HBase is installed. However, there is no guarantee that it will actually work. For that, you need to use the `status` command.

To go a little deeper in to the shell, you can follow our Hadoop illuminated labs and go through our introductory section at https://github.com/hadoop-illuminated/HI-labs/tree/master/hadoop-dev/hadoop-intro.

The shell allows you to do the following:

- View the Hadoop daemons running on your system
- Learn how to view which daemons are running
- Examine the web interfaces for the **NameNode** and **JobTracker** daemons

Now, you can experiment with the following commands:

- `status`: The `status` command is your first friend. It tells you whether HBase is running and also tells you about all the active servers:

  ```
  hbase(main):001:0> status
  1 servers, 0 dead, 13.0000 average load
  ```

  This is where you will see something that is not working first, in case your HBase is not set up correctly.

  Now, list the tables, as follows:

  ```
  hbase(main):002:0> list
  TABLE
  kiji.default.meta
  kiji.default.schema_hash
  kiji.default.schema_id
  kiji.default.system
  mytable
  users
  wordcount
  ```

```
7 row(s) in 0.0390 seconds
```

```
hbase(main):003:0>
```

As you can see, I have a number of `kiji` tables as well as regular ones that I have created. **Kiji** is a popular open source framework to jump-start your HBase modeling and development, and it is supported by a company, **WibiData**. We will talk about them in due time.

The best way to deal with the values in HBase is by creating the tables, adding values, and reading them. In the following section, we will show you how to do this.

- `create`: The `create` command creates a table as follows:

```
create 'table_name', 'fam1'
```

This command creates a table called `table_name`, with one column family named `fam1`.

You can add some values in HBase in the following format:

```
put<table name><row key><column_family : column><value>
```

Consider the following example:

```
hbase(main):016:0> put 'table_name', 'row1', 'fam1:col1', 'val1'
hbase(main):017:0> put 'table_name', 'row1', 'fam1:col2', 'val2'
hbase(main):017:0> put 'table_name', 'row2', 'fam:col1', 'val3'
```

- `scan`: The `scan` command is used to scan tables as follows:

```
hbase(main):019:0> scan 'table_name'
```

Observe the output, which might look similar to the following:

```
    ROW                              COLUMN+CELL
r1                          column=fam1:col1,
timestamp=1365320206055, value=val1
r1                          column=fam1:col2,
timestamp=1365320238460, valueval2
r2                          column=fam1:col1,
timestamp=1365320505407, value=val3    2 row(s) in 0.0420 seconds
```

Now is the time to write some simple Java code to read/write (but don't despair if you do not know Java; there is also SQL coming up).

Here is the code that will run for you:

```
package com.hi.hbase.book.chapter2;
;
// import - see GitHub for complete source code
/**
 * before running this, create '' table
 */
```

The following class will insert the user information into the pre-existing users table:

```
public class UserInsert
{

    //static String tableName = "users";
static String tableName = "users";
static String familyName = "info";

public static void main(String[] args) throws Exception
    {
    // open connection just once and re-user it
        Configuration config = HBaseConfiguration.create();
try (HTablehtable = new HTable(config, tableName)) {
int total = 100;
long t1 = System.currentTimeMillis();
        // loop to insert users value, which we are
 creating
        // later we will do better user simulation
for (inti=0; i< total ; i++)
            {
int userid = i;
            String email = "user-" + i + "@foo.com";
            String phone = "555-1234";

byte [] key = Bytes.toBytes(userid);
            Put put = new Put (key);

put.add(Bytes.toBytes(familyName), Bytes.toBytes("email"),
Bytes.toBytes(email));  // <-- email goes here
put.add(Bytes.toBytes(familyName), Bytes.toBytes("phone"),
Bytes.toBytes(phone));  // <-- phone goes here
htable.put(put);

        }
```

```
long t2 = System.currentTimeMillis();
System.out.println ("inserted " + total + " users  in " +
(t2-t1) + " ms");
        }
    }
}
```

Having run the preceding code, try to scan the data in the Hbase shell. You should get 100 values. The complete project is on GitHub at https://github.com/elephantscale/hbase-book. You can open it in your IDE such as NetBeans, Eclipse, or IDEA and run it there.

Maven is a powerful system used to build a project with all code dependencies. Our projects can be built in two ways—with a simple build script found in the labs, as we have seen in this chapter, or with a Maven command.

You can also run the project on a command line, as follows:

`mvn clean install`

This will compile and build the project, and also run all the tests.

Now that we have written the data to HBase, let's run more code in order to read it, as follows:

```
package com.hi.hbase.book.chapter2;


// required imports

This class reads the data from the user table

public class UserQuery {

    static String tableName = " users";

static String familyName = "info";

public static void main(String[] args) throws Exception {
        Configuration config = HBaseConfiguration.create();
HTablehtable = new HTable(config, tableName);
    // do as much or as little quering as you want, time it
int total = 100;
        Random rand = new Random();
for (int i = 0; i<total; i++) {
int id = rand.nextInt(total * 2);
```

```
System.out.println("querying for userId : " + id);
byte[] key = Bytes.toBytes(id);

long t1 = System.nanoTime();
        Get get = new Get(key);
long t2 = System.nanoTime();
        Result result = htable.get(get);
if (result.isEmpty()) {
            // first check, this row may not exist
System.out.println("    row user=" + id + " : not found");
        } else {
    // You always access the data through binary key
byte[] family = Bytes.toBytes(familyName);
byte[] emailCol = Bytes.toBytes("email");
KeyValuekv = result.getColumnLatest(family, emailCol);
if (kv == null) {
            // even if row exist, this column may not
exist
System.out.println("    column 'email' not found");
        } else {
        // found
byte[] value = kv.getValue();
        String email = new String(value);
System.out.println("    email=" + email);
        }
      }
System.out.println("    query time : " + (t2 - t1) / 1000000.0 +
  " ms\n");
    }
  }
}
```

The preceding code will run, and it will give you output similar to that shown in the following code. Some users will be found and some not, and that is exactly what we want to test:

```
querying for userId : 197
row user=197 : not found
query time : 0.018413 ms

querying for userId : 148
row user=148 : not found
query time : 0.003088 ms

querying for userId : 178
```

```
row user=178 : not found
query time : 0.004097 ms

querying for userId : 83
    email=user-83@foo.com
query time : 0.003783 ms

querying for userId : 7
    email=user-7@foo.com
query time : 0.003616 ms

querying for userId : 129
row user=129 : not found
query time : 0.003506 ms
```

However, this is all just done to check your ammo. In order to have a clear picture of the HBase design patterns, we should describe it in a clear, unambiguous, precise language, and what language would be better for querying databases than SQL.

A question might arise that HBase is a NoSQL database. This means that it does not understand SQL. Well, that was a while back. Nowadays, NoSQL means *Not Only SQL*.

Project Phoenix — a SQL for HBase

Phoenix is a relatively recent project that represents a SQL layer over HBase. Its blog is at `http://phoenix-hbase.blogspot.com/`, and it was first announced at this blog on January 30, 2013.

Here is a brief list of only some of the capabilities that it gives you:

- Phoenix allows columns to be modeled as a multi-part row key or key/value cells
- It provides full query support with predicate pushdown and optimal scan key formation
- It provides DDL support (CREATE TABLE, DROP TABLE, and ALTER TABLE) to add/remove columns
- It provides DML support, UPSERT VALUES for row-by-row insertion, UPSERT SELECT for mass data transfer between the same or different tables, and DELETE for deleting rows

Most importantly, it does not provide these features at the expense of performance. No, it uses a very smart query analyzer that allows the query to focus exactly on the rows that are needed, and shaves off the unnecessary data.

Now, you can understand why I want you to use it. Just as **MongoDB** is very popular because it has a SQL-like shell, and in fact you can try it online at `http://try.mongodb.org/`, and just as Cassandra introduced CQL just a couple of years ago at `http://cassandra.apache.org/doc/cql/CQL.html`, Phoenix too brings the expressiveness of SQL to HBase. In fact, you can even use it from your Java code again, just as Cassandra uses JDBC-like Java drivers with **DataStax**.

The following lines have been adopted from Shakespeare's A Midsummer Night's Dream:

> *'Ladies,'--or 'Fair-ladies--I would wish You,'--or 'I would request you,'--or 'I would entreat you,--not to fear, not to tremble: my life for yours.*

So, we follow the same pattern and we will describe our HBase design patterns with SQL coming from Phoenix. Now, just the last two steps are remaining—install Phoenix and try it, and run it from Java, just to prove the point.

Installing Phoenix

Phoenix comes to us from the **SalesForce.com** developers, and its main site is found on **GitHub** at `https://github.com/forcedotcom/phoenix`. It also features a very nicely formatted `README.md` file, something one can learn from.

Let's go ahead and install it. Here are the instructions:

1. Download and expand the installation TAR file.

   In my case, it looks like this:

   ```
   mark@mark-7:~/ThirdParty$ ll
   -rw-rw-r--  1 mark mark 17111040 Jan 10 13:29 libpst-0.6.63.tar
   -rw-r--r--  1 mark mark 18603115 Dec 26 11:41 phoenix-2.2.2-
   client.jar
   -rw-r--r--  1 mark mark  1546579 Dec 26 11:41 phoenix-2.2.2.jar
   -rw-r--r--  1 mark mark   586849 Dec 26 11:41 phoenix-2.2.2-tests.
   jar
   ```

2. Copy the Phoenix JAR file into the HBase `lib` directory of every RegionServer.

   In this case, it is as follows:

   `sudocp phoenix-2.2.2.jar /usr/lib/hbase/lib/`

   Now, check that it works with the following command:

   `hbase classpath`

   After running the command, restart the RegionServer. It will tell you whether the `.jar` file is there:

   `sudo service hbase-regionserver restart`

3. Add the Phoenix client JAR file to the classpath of your HBase client.

   I have already added Phoenix to the projects of the book's `pom.xml` file (using the instruction at `https://github.com/forcedotcom/phoenix`), and I have also copied the `phoenix-2.2.2-client.jar` file to the `lib` directory of the project for future use.

4. Download and set up **SQuirrel** as your SQL client so that you can issue an ad hoc SQL query against your HBase cluster.

   Here is a screenshot illustrating the installation of SQuirrel:

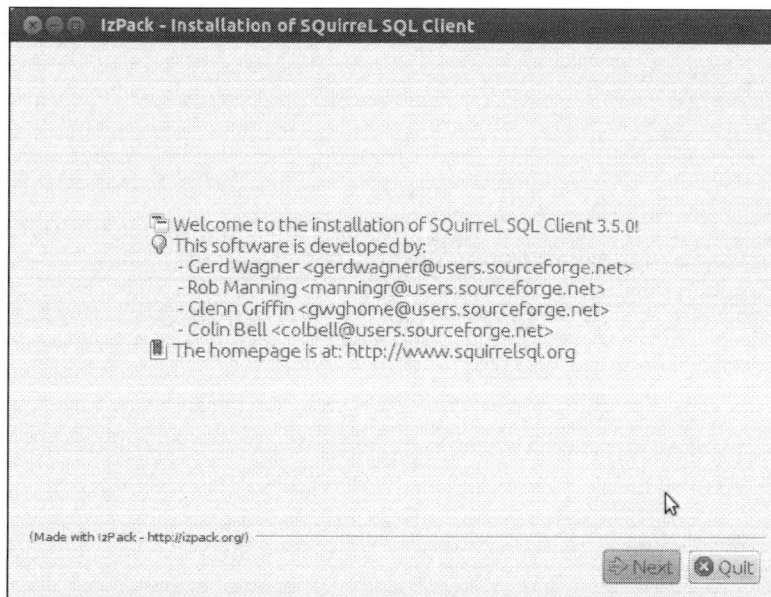

The next screenshot is SQuirrel's main window. Here, you can issue the SQL queries for HBase and see the results of your actions.

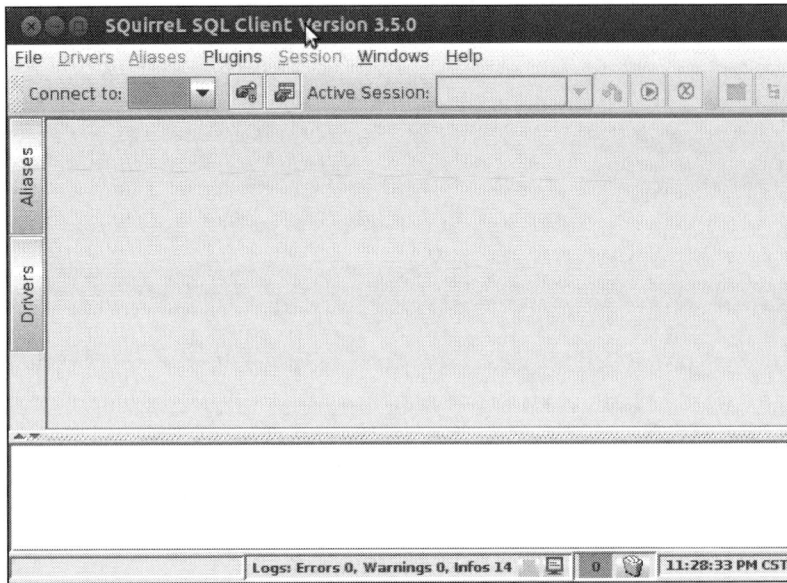

Now, add the Phoenix driver, by browsing to the appropriate JAR:

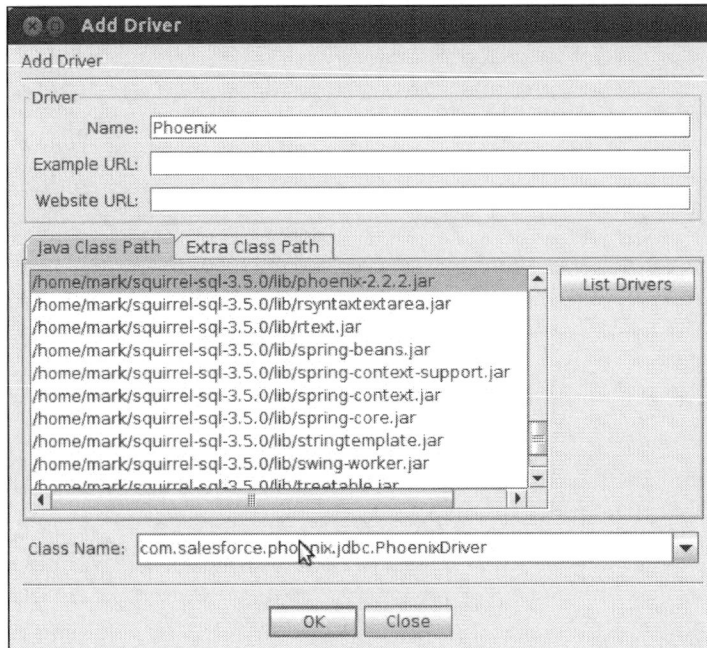

Now, go to the Phoenix shell and perform the following step:

```
mark@mark-7:~/ThirdParty/bin$ ./sqlline.sh localhost
34/34 (100%) Done
0: jdbc:phoenix:localhost>
```

To exit from the Phoenix shell, type the following command (nothing else works):

```
!quit.
```

Let's test some more examples:

```
mark@mark-7:~/ThirdParty/bin$ ./sqlline.sh localhost
../examples/stock_symbol.sql
34/34 (100%) Done
+------------+------------+
|  SYMBOL    |  COMPANY   |
+------------+------------+
|  CRM       | SalesForce.com |
+------------+------------+
```

Now, we are almost ready. Here is how you can run the Java code in Phoenix. The crown jewel of JDBC, the connection line, looks like this:

```
Connection conn =
DriverManager.getConnection("jdbc:phoenix:localhost");
```

After this, your Java code treats HBase as any other SQL database.

Summary

In this chapter, we started writing Java code to read/write to HBase. We have also seen how to control HBase with the help of the HBase shell. The most important step though was our introduction to the Phoenix project, which permits SQL over HBase, a smart sort of SQL at that. It allows you to operate through SQL statements in a manner familiar to all SQL database users. It also allows you to read/write in a more standard way even when you use Java code. Since SQL is the lingua franca of the database world, we have laid the foundation to explain the HBase design principles in a simple and easy manner.

In the next chapter, we will do a number of enhancements. We will give you the **power user** way of addressing Phoenix, and show you how easy it makes things. With this, we will be able to introduce the first design pattern.

3

Using HBase Tables for Single Entities

In this chapter, you will learn about the first actual HBase design pattern — correctly storing information in the table that reflects single entities. This will include the following topics:

- Forming row keys
- Why you should not generate keys with the database
- How and when to use collections
- Using Phoenix further

Since this is the first design pattern, I would like to acknowledge the help of my numerous colleagues, and in particular Patrick McFadin, for explaining the topics to me. I did not invent anything, but absorbed the information and am now transmitting this knowledge.

Storing user information

Imagine that you are building a scalable website to upload and view videos. The first thing you would need to do is store information about your users. However, what information do you want from your users? You will need their username, real name, e-mail or even multiple e-mails, and most likely, you would also need to store the date the user registered on your site.

Let's provide the table definition and explain how and why we will use the HBase elements. Since we have already introduced the convenient SQL way of dealing with HBase using project Phoenix, we will continue to do so from this chapter onward.

A solution for storing user information

Unlike Cassandra, HBase does not have the concept of a keyspace, database, or schema in the **relational database management system (RDBMS)** sense of the word. Therefore, all the table names have to be unique. This is not a big limitation because you can use compound table names, for example, `sujee_users`. For simplicity, we can just create the `users` table.

However, with Phoenix, we are back to having what amounts to the database/schema in RDBMS and keyspace in Cassandra. How so? Since Phoenix stores all of the table's metadata in the table itself, it can reintroduce the keyspace. Thus, we can define our table as `my_schema.my_table`.

In our case, we will be defining `my_schema.users`.

Here is the definition for the first iteration:

```
CREATE TABLE my_schema.users (
    username varchar primary key,
    firstname varchar,
    lastname varchar,
    email varchar,
    password varchar,
    created_date timestamp
);
```

Try to run this with the following script:

```
create_table_users.sh
```

Now, enter the Phoenix shell, as follows:

```
./sqlline.sh localhost
```

Then, run the following command:

```
0: jdbc:phoenix:localhost> !columns my_schema.users
```

On running the command, you will get the description of the table you just created, like this:

TABLE_CAT	TABLE_SCHEM	TABLE_NAME	COLUMN_NAME	DATA_TYPE	TYPE_NAME
null	MY_SCHEMA	USERS	USERNAME	12	VARCHAR
_0	MY_SCHEMA	USERS	FIRSTNAME	12	VARCHAR
_0	MY_SCHEMA	USERS	LASTNAME	12	VARCHAR
_0	MY_SCHEMA	USERS	EMAIL	12	VARCHAR
_0	MY_SCHEMA	USERS	PASSWORD	12	VARCHAR
_0	MY_SCHEMA	USERS	CREATED_DATE	93	TIMESTAMP

Now, let's discuss each element in `CREATE TABLE my_schema.users` and why we made it the way we did. First, the field describing the key:

```
username varchar primary key
```

You might be surprised to find that the primary key is an element of the actual data and not an artificially generated entity. However, generated keys are bad.

Here is why every NoSQL developer knows Brewer's CAP theorem, which states that you cannot have consistency (c), availability (a), and partition tolerance (p) all at the same time in a distributed database. By consistency, we mean that all the nodes in a distributed data see the same data at all times. Don't laugh, I have seen systems that give you a different answer depending on the node you ask about. This is bad enough for a social site and quite intolerable for a financial system.

Availability refers to the quality of a system that is used to give an answer in a reasonable time interval. If it can't, it should fail outright. In no case do we want a hanging system and deadlocks.

Finally, partition tolerance implies that the system keeps on operating even when parts of it fail.

In terms of the CAP theorem, HBase is a CP-type system, one that stresses on consistency and partition tolerance (for example, refer to `http://en.wikipedia.org/wiki/Apache_HBase`). This is to say that HBase is highly available. HBase, after all, runs behind Facebook. However, in the world of NoSQL, HBase is considered as emphasizing on consistency and partitioning over availability. Now, let's apply this theory to generate keys in the database.

If you ask the database to generate the key, then which part of it are you asking? You might have some servers placed close to you and the rest placed remotely, and you are asking the database to generate a unique sequence key. Obviously, you are asking for consistency. If so, availability will suffer and your key generation will become a bottleneck. So, by the nature of things, we are forced to generate our primary key.

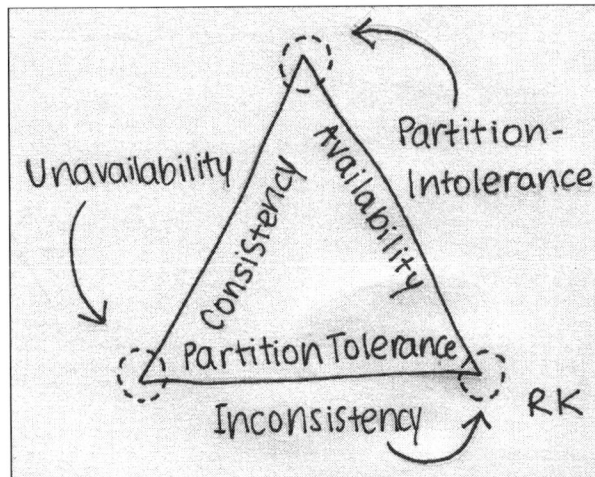

Then, we realize that this is not all that bad. In our case, the username is unique and fulfills the role of the primary key perfectly. You might ask how can one generate a username that is unique? It can also happen that two users are creating their profiles simultaneously and are trying to create the same username. In this case, while checking whether the username exists, both users will first get an answer in the negative and consequently proceed to create the same username at the same time!

The answer to this question is given by the `checkAndPut` function in the `Table` interface. This call allows you to put a new row in while checking for the existence of certain columns. The operation is atomic, and one of the users will get the `name already exists` error.

Thus, the need for generating a unique key in this case is solved. In later chapters, we will discuss more techniques that will tell you how to generate primary keys by yourself without relying on the database to do this for you. You will learn to appreciate this new habit.

> For the lists of values, use the `SQL ARRAY` construct.

But wait! Users usually have one username, but they might very well have multiple e-mail addresses. So, what we want is list of e-mails. Execute the following query to get a list of e-mails:

```
CREATE TABLE my_schema.users (
...
    email list varchar,
...
);
```

While there is no list in HBase, Phoenix introduces a SQL array. Here is your table definition:

```
CREATE TABLE my_schema.users (
    username varchar primary key,
    firstname varchar,
    lastname varchar,
    email varchar[],
    password varchar,
    created_date timestamp
);
```

Please note the use of `email varchar[]` for the definition of the array. Now you can store as many emails as you want. What is especially nice is that you can avoid the use of fields such as `email1`, `email2`, `email3`, and so on, which leave much to be desired. There is no way to reorder e-mails in one operation; for example, some people might have five or even ten emails and they might run out of fields, while some have only one and might waste the space.

With pure lists, you can prepend and append items to the list, while in HBase Phoenix, you can only set, read, or write the whole array. However, this is good enough to store emails.

The `SQL ARRAY` functionality exists in Phoenix, starting with the 3.0 release. If you are unable to find a ready release to download, you can clone it from GitHub and build it yourself. That is what I have done. At this point, I would like to thank the Phoenix team for providing me with the help and documentation at the time of writing.

Sets, maps, and lists

HBase and Phoenix are under constant development. While sets, maps, and lists' features are not complete right now, they might be included by the time you read this book. For now, we have implemented these in our companion code on GitHub.

Generating the test data

Ideally, we would like to generate data in order to be able to test our solution. Here too, Phoenix comes to the rescue because it allows us to generate SQL statements that can then be executed. The code to do this is found in HDPP at `https://github.com/markkerzner/hbase-book/blob/master/src/main/java/com/elephantscale/hbase/book/chapter3/GenerateUsers.java` under the `GenerateUsers.java` file.

The following is the main method for date generation:

```
public static void main(String argv[]) {
  if (argv.length != 2) {
    System.out.println("Arguments: number-users, number-emails-per-
user");
    System.exit(0);
  }
  GenerateUsers generator = new GenerateUsers();
  int nUsers = Integer.parseInt(argv[0]);
  int nEmails = Integer.parseInt(argv[1]);
  try {
```

```
      generator.generate(nUsers, nEmails);
    } catch (Exception e) {
      System.out.println("Problem writig files: " + e.getMessage());
      e.printStackTrace(System.out);
    }
  }
}
```

As you can see, the main method simply collects two arguments and passes them on to the `generate()` method. It also explains the usage and gives an explanatory error message when the usage is not observed.

The key code fragment is the `generate()` method and it starts by preparing the output directory like this:

```
private void generate(int nUsers, int nEmails) throws IOException {
        SimpleDateFormat dateFormat = new SimpleDateFormat
("yyyy-MM-dd HH:mm:ss");
        new File(Util.ROOT_DIR).mkdirs();
        Charset charset = Charset.forName("US-ASCII");
        if (nEmails < 1) {
            nEmails = 1;
        }
```

The most important loop to generate is the users. Here it is:

```
for (int u = 1; u <= nUsers; ++u) {
  StringBuilder insert = new StringBuilder();
  insert.append("INSERT INTO users (username, firstname, lastname,
email, password, created_date) VALUES (");
  String firstName = util.generateName();
  String lastName = util.generateName();
  String username = firstName + lastName;
        insert.append("'").append(username).append("','").
append("'").
append(firstName).append("','").append("'").append(lastName).
append("','");
  insert.append("[");
  for (int e = 0; e < nEmails; ++e) {
            insert.append("'").append(util.generateName()).
append("@").
append(util.generateDomain()).append("'");
    if (e < nEmails - 1) {
    insert.append(",");
    }
  }
  insert.append("],");
```

```
    insert.append("'").append(util.generateName()).append("',");
    insert.append("'").append(dateFormat.format(
new Date())).append("');").append("\n");
    Files.append(insert.toString(), new File(userFile), charset);
 }
```

Please note that in the internal loop, we generate a random number of emails for users. The code for all random generation e-mails is collected in the `Util` class.

To actually use this code, generate the data and prefill the table. Then enter the following command:

cd generators

./run_generate_users.sh 100 10

Here, the two parameters are `number-users` and `number-emails` per user. This will generate the required number of rows in the `generated` folder.

Now, run the following command to load the data:

./sqlline.sh localhost $HBASE_BOOK_HOME/generated/users.txt

Analyzing your query

In order to analyze a query, we need to pay attention to performance monitoring for each query. Phoenix lacks the profiling feature, but there is a lot of work going on in this direction. Meanwhile, you can analyze the steps needed in order to perform the query. This is described at `http://phoenix.incubator.apache.org/language/index.html#/explain`. By analyzing the steps of a query, we can reason the performance of that query. In this case, the steps are simple enough to understand and are left for the reader to work with in the form of an exercise.

Exercise

Insert a username and then insert it again. Watch the overwriting without any warning. How will you place a new e-mail at the top or bottom of the list?

As an added exercise, please come up with your answers before looking at the answer provided.

Solution

Insert the user data using the following query:

```
INSERT INTO users
(username, firstname, lastname, email, password, created_date)
VALUES ('johnsmith', 'John', 'Smith', ['johnsmith@gmail.com',
'johnsmith@yahoo.com'], 'password123', '2013-09-09');
INSERT INTO users
(username, firstname, lastname, email, password, created_date)
VALUES ('johnsmith', 'John', 'Smith', ['johnsmith@gmail.com',
'johnsmith@yahoo.com'], 'password123', '2013-09-09');
```

Now, prepend an e-mail like this:

```
UPDATE users SET email = ['me@johnsmith.com'] + email WHERE username
= 'johnsmith';
```

Then, you can append the e-mail at the end as follows:

```
UPDATE users SET email = email + ['me@johnsmith.com'] WHERE username
= 'johnsmith';
```

Analyze your queries using the `explain` command (for more details, go to http://phoenix.incubator.apache.org/language/index.html#/explain.)

What does the `explain` command do? It computes the logical steps necessary to execute the given command. This is similar to the execution plan you will find in SQL databases. Each step is then represented as a string in a single-column result set row.

Summary

In this chapter, we learned how to design tables for simple single entities. The key notions here were how and when to generate HBase rows' keys, why sequence key generation is an antipattern, how to use the lists of values in your schema, and how to make Phoenix's SQL array do the work for you.

In the next chapter, we will look at the principles of storing time series data, how to avoid the pitfalls characteristic of this type of problem, and how to use best practices that can help guarantee performance and scalability of HBase.

4
Dealing with Large Files

Large files present a special challenge for any database, such as SQL or NoSQL, and HBase is no exception to this. This is because databases were not designed for large files in the first place. Rather, they were designed to store column values in rows (which are usually small strings or numbers).

Gradually, the use of databases was expanded and strings became longer. Then, people wanted to store binary information (just because there was no other convenient place to store it) so that they could point to one location and say with confidence, "This is where all my data lives." Thus came the concept of a **binary large object (BLOB)**.

However, again, since no database was designed to store large objects, you would have to design a custom solution based on your requirements, that is, the size of the objects, the frequency of reads and writes, and so on.

We will approach this chapter in the following manner:

- Discuss the keys for storing large files
- Discuss how and where to store large files
- What are the possible solutions?
- What are the advantages and disadvantages of each of these solutions?
- What are the performance parameters when the solution begins to deteriorate?
- Who uses what?

  Even though some companies' solutions might not be available as open source code, we can always benefit by learning from them.

Let's discuss each point by proceeding in the order we just listed.

Storing files using keys

Each file that you want to store as an object in HBase needs to be stored using a key. We will also retrieve it using this key. Where do you get these keys from?

We have already discussed why we should not ask the database to generate these keys in *Chapter 3, Using HBase Tables for Single Entities*. There, we said that a database is distributed. So, if you have consistent key generation, it will become a bottleneck. If you distribute your key generation, the keys will either be inconsistent or the central management of the keys will slow down HBase. In *Chapter 3, Using HBase Tables for Single Entities*, we found a solution for the specific case under discussion — since our usernames had to be unique, by the nature of the requirements, we simply used the username as a unique key.

This is not ideal, however. Firstly, it is not generic, and secondly, it is out of our control and might lead to a database imbalance (as we will discuss in *Chapter 5, Time Series Data*). Therefore, now is a good time to introduce a general solution for the key generation problem — the use of **UUID**.

Using UUID

A **universally unique identifier (UUID)** is an identifier standard that is used in software construction, standardized by the **Open Software Foundation (OSF)** as part of the **distributed computing environment (DCE)**. On Microsoft Windows platforms, it is known as a **globally unique identifier (GUID)**.

The lesson that we learn here is that UUID is a prime citizen in the NoSQL world.

Why do we need it? We want to enable distributed systems to uniquely identify information without significant central coordination.

Please note that unique means *practically unique* rather than *guaranteed unique*. Since the identifiers have a finite size, it is possible for two different items to share the same identifier.

Today, in the life of an HBase developer using Java, generating UUIDs is easy. Here is a code snippet that lets you do this:

```
import java.util.UUID;
String my_uuid = UUID.randomUUID().toString();
```

Once you generate the UUID, you can use it to store the large files, or any HBase row for that matter.

What follows next is an example of a small program generating the UUIDs, just to give you a feel for them (taken from http://www.portablefreeware.com/?id=2042):

Now, in your HBase application, you can use something similar to this code fragment:

```
byte [] key = UUID.randomUUID().toString();
Put put = new Put (key);
put.add(Bytes.toBytes(familyName), Bytes.toBytes("email"),
Bytes.toBytes(email));
put.add(Bytes.toBytes(familyName), Bytes.toBytes("phone"),
Bytes.toBytes(phone));
```

This code allows each client to generate a key and to store the data in HBase using this key, without worrying about possible key collisions with the other clients who are generating their keys.

That is, in the case of storing user information, if you are storing files, you will probably use the following code:

```
byte[] bytedata = Files.toByteArray(file);
byte [] key = UUID.randomUUID().toString();
Put put = new Put (key);
put.add(Bytes.toBytes(familyName), Bytes.toBytes("phone"),
bytedata);
```

This code generates the key in the same way; then, it reads all of the file's bytes and stores them in an HBase cell.

What to do when your binary files grow larger

As mentioned, we are going to progress from simple to more complex solutions. The code we just saw is good for small binary files. Most developers, as well as the HBase documentation, will tell you that here we are talking about megabytes (not even 10 MB to 50 MB). You will have to experiment with your solution and vary the data size. However, what if you find the database to be too slow?

There are a few approaches that you can take.

Using Google Blobstore to store large files

Google BlobStore is described at `https://developers.google.com/appengine/docs/java/blobstore/overview`. This is a service that Google gives you, the developer. It is called the **Blobstore** API. It allows your application to serve data objects, called **blobs**, that are much larger than the size allowed for objects in the **datastore** service. Blobs are useful for serving large files, such as video files or image files, and for allowing users to upload large data files. Naturally, you can use it only if you are allowed to use Google App Engine as part of your solution.

Facebook's Haystack for the storage of large files

Facebook's Haystack is described at `http://www.facebook.com/note.php?note_id=76191543919`. The Haystack paper describes all the design considerations and the implementations that you will have to perform in order to store large files in your system. You need to think of the read/write loads and of the hardware on which you will run it. Most likely, you don't need all the bells and whistles of Haystack and can implement a simpler solution. Alas! Haystack is not available as open source.

Twitter solution to store large files

Twitter's solution for this problem is published at `https://blog.twitter.com/2012/blobstore-twitter%E2%80%99s-house-photo-storage-system`. Twitter needs to store pictures and photographs. Today, you can hardly expect people to read anything unless it is supplied with a picture. Take my own blog, `http://mkerzner.blogspot.com/`, for example. If while explaining the most complex law one can also enjoy the world's best art, it becomes fun and educational at the same time. So, Twitter needs to store millions of photos, and they have had to design their own solution.

As always, each such solution answers a specific set of design goals, and the lesson we learn here is to define our design goals, understanding that they might well be different from anybody else's. Here are the advantages of using Twitter's solution:

- **Low cost**: This reduces the amount of money and time spent to store large files

- **High performance**: This serves images in the low tens of milliseconds, while maintaining a throughput of hundreds and thousands of requests per second

- **Easy to operate**: This lets you scale the operational overhead with continuously growing infrastructure

Accordingly, Twitter created their own solution with everything in it, that is, redundant storage, multiserver communication through ZooKeeper (`http://zookeeper.apache.org/`), and fast serving of the images.

Amazon S3 storage for very large objects

Amazon stores billions of objects with a redundant and fault-tolerant **S3** system. The design is proprietary and is not widely publicized. However, it is given as a service and can be used as such.

Please note that Amazon S3 is also a key-value store and delivers the same functionality as Google BlobStorage. Again, you can use it only if you are allowed to use Amazon's AWS as a part of your solution. It might make more sense than you might have initially imagined, as cloud-based storage is fault-tolerant, simple, and reliable. It can be expensive for large files, and you might not have enough bandwidth for you. So much for S3.

A practical approach

Now is the time for the less fancy and more practical approaches that you can implement yourself. You can store the URL (the HDFS URL) in HBase and the actual file in the HDFS. This approach gives you the data tolerance of HDFS, since the data is replicated three times by default in HDFS.

Here is what your logical data structure might look like in this approach:

File ID (UUID)	File display name	File URL of access
`f81d4fae-7dec-11d0-a765-00a0c91e6bf6`	My cat movie	`/user/storage/pic1.mp4`

This does feel a little crude, doesn't it? However, this is a design pattern that has been around since the birth of SQL databases, and it worked. Considering the fact that HDFS is unlimited in size and is fault-tolerant and self-healing, it can work even better here.

Finally, you can look for your own library or you can design it such that it stores multiple small blocks comprising of large files, each one in HBase. Now, I have not found such a library, and it will face the usual problem of hiding the complexities of a big data system, which aim for scalability. Here is what I mean—big data is complex. Just because you created a nice library and your developers like it, it does not automatically mean that they will use it in the most efficient way. Since all of big data is about performance, you might have to formulate a set of best practices, with examples, so that your elegant solution will deliver elegant performance. Otherwise, the developer might not know how to use it efficiently, and because of this, it might be inefficient.

Here are the possible problems with storing somewhat large files in HBase (just to warn you):

- HBase periodically compacts it's entire index on disk to provide efficient random lookups against this index. The compaction of large files might be very inefficient. In essence, they are already compacted, since many video formats provide compression. Yet, your database will be rewriting them to a different place, trying to squeeze out more performance, but in fact, just moving files around.

- Committing a (large) blob to disk will be unnecessarily expensive. Firstly, the entire blob will be written once to the commit log, and then it will be written out again to the actual HBase file. Each of these writes will be replicated three times by HDFS. Also, remember that you might want to write to another data center too. Unnecessary duplication could thus cost a lot.

Practical recommendations

In your actual work, use the following multistep approach. Use the simple approach if it works, and if not, go to a more complex one.

If the file is small, store it in HBase (make this threshold a parameter, as you might want to experiment with it).

Store the file path in HBase, together with the description and the actual file, in HDFS.

Implement your own library that breaks files into small manageable pieces and stores or retrieves them for you.

A practical lab

Let's walk through an application that gives you a practical case of large files—a video site. Suppose you need to store your videos and describe them in an appropriate HBase table, and you have already chosen to store the videos elsewhere, not in your database. How will you design your table?

> At this point, I will encourage you to close the book and design your table. Then, come back and compare your design with the one I give you.

So, we need to store many videos for a unique user. You already know that we decided not to store the video itself, for purely technical reasons. There are other reasons also, which we have mentioned here:

- The video is not a part of the `videos` table because its entry in the table might be ready when the video is not.

- Your performance profiling and debugging will be messed up if you combine the big and small data pieces.

- Anyway, it is usually stored in a **content delivery network** (**CDN**) because it is a better and more practical way of video delivery. (You can read more about CDN at `http://en.wikipedia.org/wiki/Content_delivery_network`.)

With this, here's my table description in terms of SQL, as enabled by Phoenix:

```
//  Entity table that will store many videos for a unique user
CREATE TABLE videos (
    videoid uuid,
    videoname varchar,
    username varchar,
    description varchar,
    location map<varchar,varchar>,
    tags set<varchar>,
    upload_date timestamp,
    PRIMARY KEY (videoid)
);
```

Here are specific points to note about this code:

- `videoid uuid`: We already mentioned that UUID is a first-class citizen in the NoSQL world. The video's name cannot be considered as a natural ID. We cannot, and should not, use sequence keys for a video ID, but using UUID on the other hand is OK.

- `username varchar`: The username belongs to one user, and it is already found in our `user` table. However, note that we duplicated the username here, rather than creating a column to join the `user` and `video` tables. That, of course, is the NoSQL design pattern to avoid joins. The username is what we will need when we query the table, so we will put it here. On queries, we will obtain both the video and the user information in one go. Had we needed more user information, we would likely put it in our `video` table also. It is true that we will need to maintain this information in both the tables, but that is exactly the point.

- `tags set<varchar>`: Really, we need a set here. Our tags are not ordered, and this should not be reflected in the structure of the field. Lists are more structured, and therefore, the implementation of a list might take a slight performance hit. However, there are no sets in Phoenix as yet, and a list is close enough to what we need here.

- `downloadurl map<varchar,varchar>`: As you can see, we made `downloadurl map<String, String>`, where the key is the region and the value is the URI of the video. That is because content delivery systems usually store the video in different regions. Once a user makes a request, we know their location by IP. From here, we can find the recommended geographical location, from all that we have available, and the map will return the URL for that location.

Exercises

Let's see how well we have understood the concepts. Next, you will find some exercises and their sample answers:

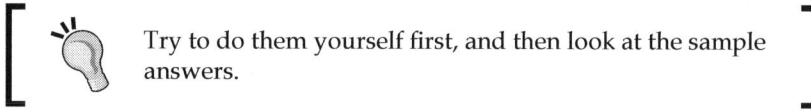

> Try to do them yourself first, and then look at the sample answers.

- Manually insert a row in the `video` table.

  The sample answer is as follows:

  ```
  INSERT INTO videos
  (videoid, videoname, username, description, location, tags,
  upload_date)
  VALUES
  (18134b9d-6222-4f0e-b06d-4ba1e6c62f50, 'my cat',
  'johnsmith', 'this is my cat', {'us' :
  'http://right.here'}, {'cats', 'pets'}, '2013-09-09
  21:33:15');
  ```

  Note that there is no UUID generator for HBase, and this one was generated with the Java code.

- Experiment with the data load.

  To generate data for this, we have provided the code in an open source project. Moreover, the project contains the JAR files that are already prebuilt and committed. So, just by cloning it, you can start using the JAR files without the need to build the code.

Thus, to generate data for performance testing, clone or download this project from `github: https://github.com/markkerzner/cas-dax-labs`. It contains the compiled JAR files, so all that you need to run it is Java.

Run this generator, for example, as follows:

```
cd generators
./run_generate_videos.sh 100 10
```

Here, the two parameters are `number-videos` and `number-locations-per-video`.

Then, you can load the generated user data. (Please consult the labs for the load script.)

To analyze the SQL, examine the `videos.txt` file.

- Add a location to a map, modify it, and delete it.

  Consider this example:

  ```
  UPDATE videos SET location = {'us' : 'http://right.there'} WHERE
  videoid = 18134b9d-6222-4f0e-b06d-4ba1e6c62f50;
  ```

- Do performance testing and profiling on your table.

  Maps are serialized, and this incurs a performance cost. Generate data with 10 locations or with 100 locations. Run it with trace turned on and find the point where the performance of this location map becomes a problem. (For more information on tracing, please consult `http://hbase.apache.org/book/tracing.client.shell.html`.) To turn on tracing, use this command:

  ```
  hbase> trace 'start'
  ```

  Now, you can run the inserts by copying and pasting the generated video's data.

  Run it with 5, 10, 20, and other such locations. When does the performance noticeably deteriorate?

  The following points should be noted on profiling:

    ◦ Observe the wealth of information you get with tracing turned on

    ◦ All of this tracing information is available with the Java API, and that is how you can approach measuring performance in production, without writing custom load testing code

    ◦ Keep in mind that tracing has its own overhead; so, use it only for debugging and profiling, not for overall performance measurements

One bonus exercise—what will you use to fix the problem of having too many maps?

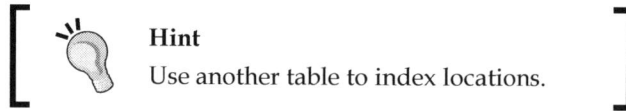

> **Hint**
> Use another table to index locations.

Send your solutions to us or post them on the book forum, which we are planning to start just after publication.

Summary

In this chapter, we dealt with the problem of storing large files in conjunction with HBase. We reviewed the known solutions in use by companies such as Google, Amazon, Facebook, and Twitter, and we also suggested lessons to be gleaned in our own implementations. We also outlined a practical approach that you can take when implementing the storage of large files in your own HBase system.

In the following chapter, we will take a look at the equally ubiquitous problem of storing time-based information in HBase and NoSQL databases. We will describe the general principles and give practical advice.

5
Time Series Data

In this chapter, we will cover the following topics:

- What we mean by time series data
- The special design challenges that time series data presents
- Which important performance considerations apply
- The best practices to consider when dealing with time series data

All of us are familiar with time series data. Although we will provide a definition and examples later, you can think of it as minute-by-minute trading data. Such data presents a number of challenges for the HBase designer, as they need to create a proper schema for the data, find a balance between convenience and performance, and also keep factors such as as the overheating of specific region servers and bloated bloom filters in mind.

If all of this sounds obscure at the moment, we will try to make it clear by the end of this chapter. As we will see, HBase is perfect for storing time series data. However, one needs to pay attention to a number of pesky details.

Let's start with a definition of time series data. Time series data is a type of data that is recorded at regular time intervals. Some examples of time series data include logs, sensor data (power grid), stock ticks, monitoring systems, and many others.

Please note that *logs* can have a few different meanings. In the modern world, when talking about logs, we are usually referring to web logs or the recording of events that happens when users browse a website and a web server sends them the pages and records their actions.

The second type of log, however, is the application log. It's a file created by an application that is executing and using a logging system. These are managed by software developers to record what is going on, for compliance reasons, and to help them debug issues.

There is another type of log too, namely the well log. This happens when a well-logging tool is pulled up the oil well and it is recording measurements such as resistivity or magnetic resonance. These are later used to analyze the formation of oil deposits and find them. This subject is dear to my heart, because I have written a book on this, *Image Processing in Well Log Analysis*, and it has recently been republished.

To summarize, there are vast varieties of time series data, and each one of them is important in its own right. Each poses a specific interesting challenge when HBase is used to store this type of data. Therefore, we will discuss the following areas that relate to time series data:

- Using time-based keys
- Avoiding region hotspotting
- Tall and narrow rows versus wide rows
- OpenTSDB principles

Using time-based keys to store time series data

The most natural key to use in order to store time series data is time (for example, in milliseconds). This is guaranteed to be unique, since this is exactly what you are recording—a measurement at a particular time. To give our example a practical flavor, let's take a look at a well log, as all well logs are perfect examples of time series data.

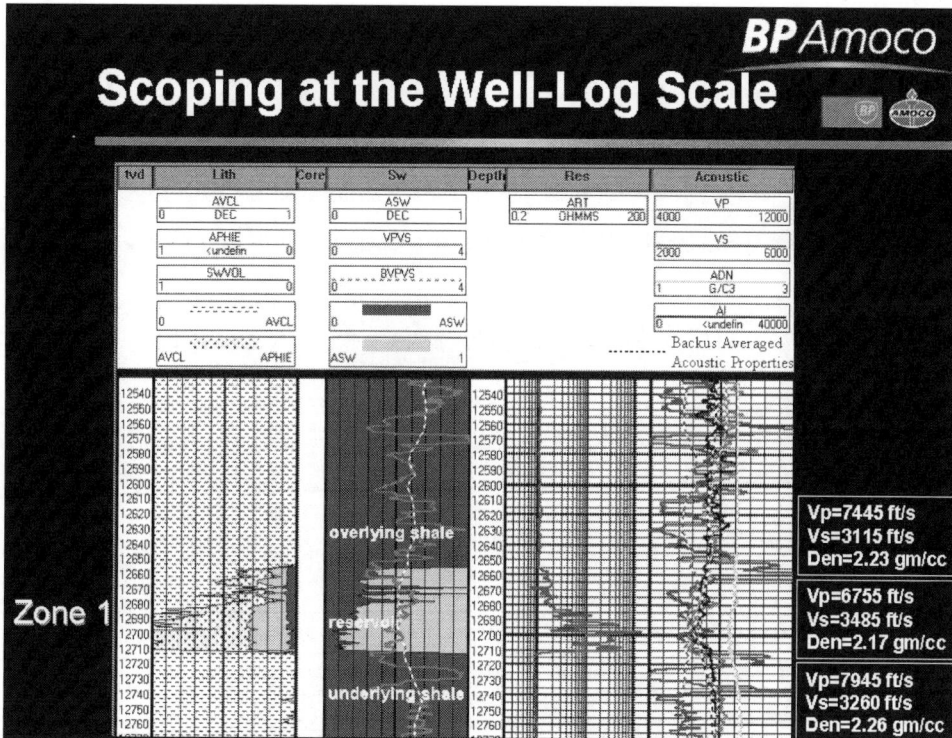

(The source of this image is Baird Petrophysical found at http://www.bairdpetro.com/ and has been used with their due permission.)

As you can see, well logs record a certain measurement (in this case, it is sonic waves) on the millisecond scale. So, let's imagine for the sake of our example that we are recording the data every millisecond, and the HBase table contents look similar to this:

Key (time, milliseconds)	Family:Column name	Family:Column name
1402282760	Logs:Lith, Logs:SW, Logs:Res	Other: Depth, Other: acceleration
1402282761	Logs:Lith, Logs:SW, Logs:Res	Other: Depth, Other: acceleration
1402282762	etc.	etc.

Okay, so this looks great and clear. You can get the data at any millisecond in one read. You can also perform a nice scan on the range of key values. Since all the rows that are stored in HBase are already sorted by key, your scans are guaranteed to be fast.

However, there are two problems with this approach. They are as follows:

- The first problem is that it can result in the overloading (overheating) of some of the region servers, because during writes, all the data is concentrated in the regions they serve and no data is recorded in the other regions. Similarly, during typical reads against the most recent data, we will be querying a small number of regions.

- The second problem with this approach is that you are storing relatively few columns in each row, and this might be very inefficient due to very little information being read at one time and due to the presence of too many bloom filter values.

Each of the potential problems can kill the performance of our application. It is, therefore, important to understand both well.

Avoiding region hotspotting

This refers to our first problem, as monotonically increasing key values are bad. Why is that?

This is very well explained by Ikai Lan, a Google engineer at the time when he wrote this explanation, and he's currently working for Developer Relations at Google NYC. Ikai was also an early inspiration for the doodles and cartoons used in this book and my other big data cartoon series, which can be found at http://shmsoft.blogspot.com/search/label/Hadoop%20cartoons, so he deserves a special acknowledgement.

When you write all the new rows sequentially, they all end up being on the same server, because they are sorted and this forces them to be close to each other. It is true that there is sharding, and moreover, there is automatic sharding. This means that the new regions (the areas of the hard drive where the data is written) will eventually come into play, but this happens only later. Right now, you have got a hotspot.

Practically, you won't notice this under low write speeds. If you have less than a hundred writes per second, this is not important since your RegionServer copes quite all right. This number (hundred writes per second) might change on your hardware and HBase, but it will be in the low range, because it means that you are not utilizing your entire HBase cluster but only one server. This is how Ikai illustrates this:

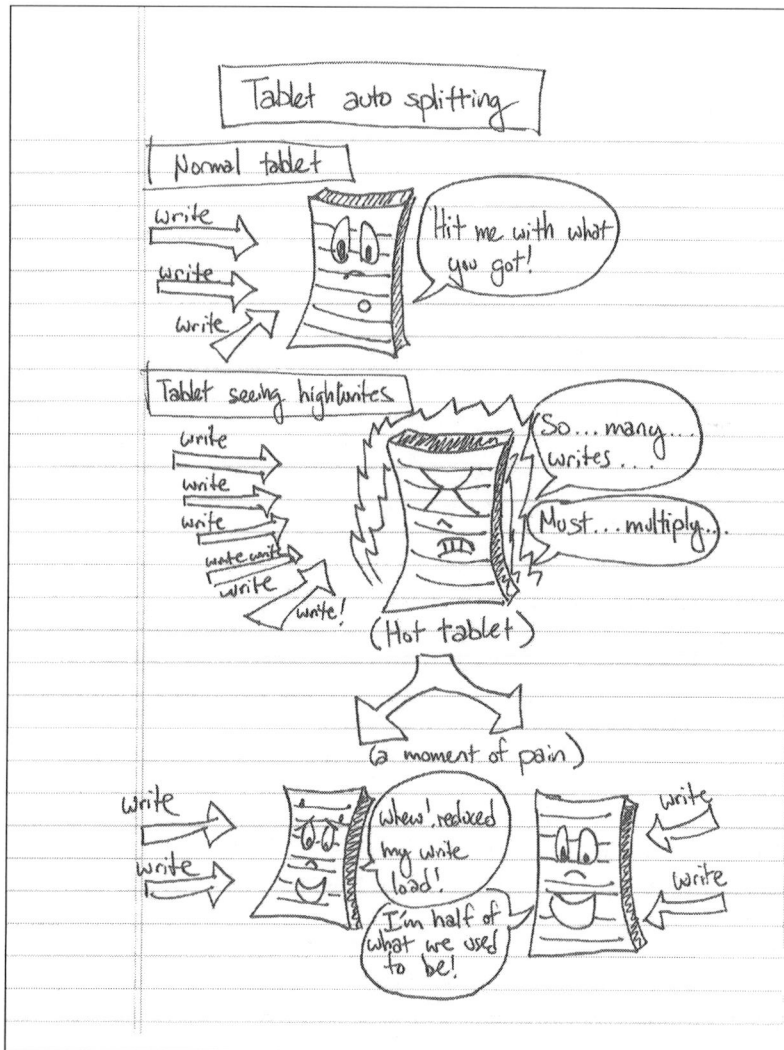

(The source of this image is `http://ikaisays.com/2011/01/25/app-engine-datastore-tip-monotonically-increasing-values-are-bad/`, and the image has been used with their due permission.)

Actually, Ikai is talking in terms of Google's BigTable, the design on which HBase is based. BigTable shards (divides the load) not only when it outgrows the region size but also when it sees a disproportionately high load on one table. As far as I know, HBase does not have such a provision. All the more, we should be careful not to concentrate our keys. So, what should you do?

You can do one of the following things:

- **Avoid indices if you can**: In your case, you will have to record the row using something else instead of time as the key. This is not the perfect approach in the case of well logs, since you need to know when the values were recorded. The depth of the measurement will give you the same problem.

- **Randomize your writes**: Even pseudorandomization will help you to offload some of the servers. Again, in our case, the sorted time is essential information; we will be hard pressed to do without it. The two pieces of advice given so far might be good for other situations (such as writing dictionary words in a random sequence), but not for true time series data. Your writes will be faster, but your reads will be slower, because you will have to collect the information from many places.

- **Prefix a shard identifier to your key**: You can distribute the load between multiple servers yourself. Now, when you are reading the data back, you will have to read it from each server, prefix all the possible server numbers to your time, and combine the query results in memory. A bit of a bother, but this will work.

The three pieces of the preceding advice are actually good, each for their own situation. It's just that for time series data, only the last one is practical. We will see how to write the code for this later in this chapter.

A partial solution to the problem can be provided by preloading, which we will discuss later. In brief, preloading, or more technically bulk loading, comes into play when you already have a lot of data to write to HBase. In this case, you can select the number of regions to be created. Then, all of them are used. If you combine this with the real read/write load, you might be lucky and your workload might already be distributed between the regions (shards) that you have previously created.

Tall and narrow rows versus wide rows

This section refers to our second problem of records being too short.

If the record that you write for one time series set is too small, you run into cache-hit problems and very large bloom filters. This is easy to understand. Hadoop reads blocks from HDFS, which usually range in size between 64 MB to 256 MB. If your data reads and writes are much smaller than this, you are bound to see inefficiencies and hence the cache-hit problems. Bloom filters answer the question—based on the key, is it possible that your data resides in the given region? The answer *no* is definite, but the answer *yes* should be understood as *maybe yes*, necessitating a read of the region and a search. If your keys are responsible for very thin rows with little information, you will have too many bloom filter keys, which will both take the hard drive space and reduce the efficiency using bloom filters in the first place.

What are the practical limits? Anything starting with the HDFS block size and ending in tens of thousands of rows. Even though, theoretically, you can have millions of columns, practical researcher Patrick McFadin reports that after tens of thousands of columns, you start eating into 95 percentiles of your read latencies and this is mostly due to deserialization costs on the larger indexes.

OpenTSDB principles

OpenTSDB is a set of tools that allow you to store and retrieve time series data. It uses HBase for data storage and retrieval, but isolates you, the user, from HBase completely. Thus, you don't have to know or care about HBase (other than administer it). To the user, it is a very simple tool, which asks them to send the time series data and then allows all kinds of displays.

We will use OpenTSDB, as promised, for two purposes:

- To teach you the use of the tool for your needs
- To elucidate on the design principles so that you can use them in your own coding, if you cannot use OpenTSDB tools directly but need a similar functionality in your application

The following diagram shows the OpenTSDB architecture:

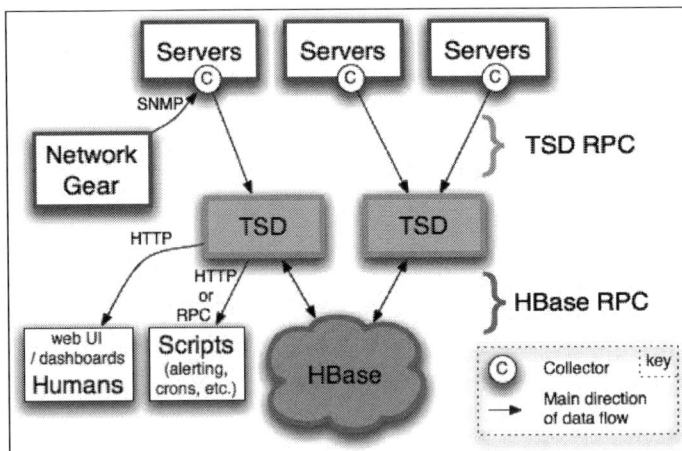

Let's first take a look at how to use the tools of OpenTSDB without any additional code development. This is what the tools allow you to do:

- Collect the data from various sources for OpenTSDB. For example, you can use any of the following provided tools:

    ○ **Vacuumetrix**: This pulls data from various cloud services or APIs and stores the results in the backend, such as Graphite, Ganglia, and OpenTSDB

    ○ **Statsd publisher**: This publishes data to TSD with StatsD

    ○ **Flume module**: This writes data from Flume to TSD

- Display the data in a nice graphical form, such as the one shown next, using **gnuplot**:

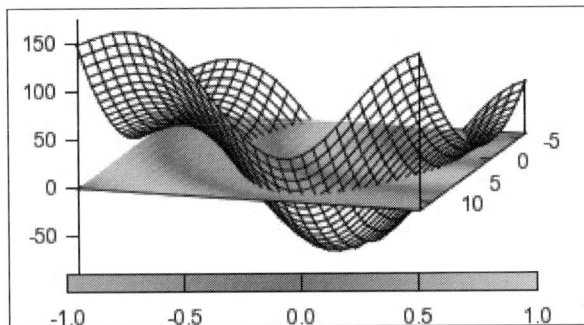

- Use the standard OpenTSDB graph, such as the one shown here, for monitoring, which is the primary OpenTSDB use case:

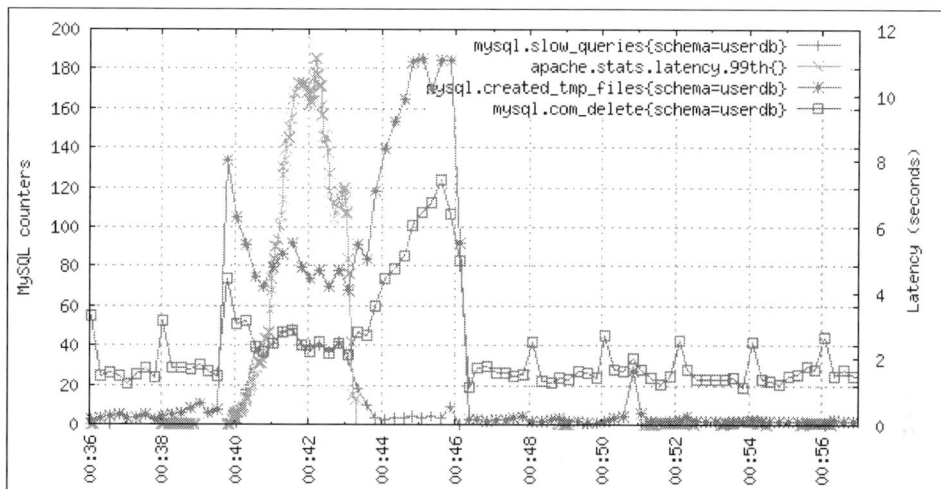

However, here we are more interested in the OpenTSDB design principles, since this shows us the experience of others rather than our limited experience. So, the designers give us those pointers (with the explanation).

The overall design of TSDB

Here are the lessons that we can glean from the overall design of TSDB. All OpenTSDB data points are stored in a single, massive table, named `tsdb` by default. This is to take advantage of HBase's ordering and region distribution. All the values are stored in the `t` column family.

The lesson that we learned here is to use a simple schema, as you will have enough complexity anyway. So, go with the recommended HBase design.

The row key

Row keys are byte arrays that comprise of the metric UID, a base timestamp, and the UID for tag key-value pairs, for example, `<metric_uid><timestamp><tagk1><tagv 1>[...<tagkN><tagvN>]`. By default, UIDs are encoded on three bytes.

The lesson that we learn here is to use composite keys, take care of load balancing by adding the UID at the beginning, put the timestamp in the key, and add additional information at the end. Note that, ordering is done inside the composite key, thus reflecting the types of queries we anticipate.

The timestamp

The timestamp is a Unix epoch value in seconds, encoded on 4 bytes. Rows are broken up into hour increments, reflected by the timestamp in each row. Thus, each timestamp will be normalized to an hour value, for example, `2013-01-01 08:00:00`. This is to avoid stuffing too many data points in a single row as that would affect region distribution. However, note that it can result in a large number of data points if the frequency of data generation is high.

Also, since HBase sorts the data on the row key, the data for the same metric and time bucket, but with different tags, will be grouped together for efficient queries. This assumes that the number of tags is small, and indeed OpenTSDB limits it to eight tags.

When storing time series data, implement the following best practices:

- Store a reasonable time interval per row. The amount of data should not make the table too tall and thin or too narrow and wide. One hour was chosen here.
- Use tags to store the time interval designation.
- Use your own data encoding, since we deal with binary data here.
- Take advantage of the natural sorting of columns in the row.
- Design for efficient access.

Compactions

Why is compaction required? The answer is to reduce the storage (as the key is repeatedly stored for each column). If compactions have been enabled for a TSD, a row might be compacted after its base hour has passed or a query has run over the row. The lesson here is that in your design, keep the compactions, both minor and major, in mind, because they will affect the performance.

The UID table schema

A separate, small table called `tsdb-uid` stores UID mappings, both forward and reverse. Two columns exist, one called `name` that maps a UID to a string and another called `id` that maps strings to UIDs.

Here, we will learn to keep the lookup tables in the same HBase. A small table can be directed to be served from the memory, so you can use HBase for its in-memory database capabilities too. Additional information can be gleaned from the OpenTSDB design documentation found at `http://opentsdb.net/docs/build/html/user_guide/backends/hbase.html`.

For practical purposes, if your NoSQL database is Cassandra and not HBase, you will find that there is a Cassandra implementation of TSDB, called **KairosDB**, which can be found at `https://code.google.com/p/kairosdb`.

Summary

We learned the important NoSQL and HBase design principles related to storing and accessing time series data. We described how to utilize time-based keys, how to avoid region hotspotting, how to properly balance tall and narrow rows versus wide rows, and we also saw how to glean additional information from other systems on top of HBase, such as OpenTSDB. All this together should make us masters at storing and using time series data in HBase and in NoSQL databases in general.

In the next chapter, we will deal with the most common design principle, that is, denormalization. We will also discuss how to store all the objects for a user, popularity contest, and how to store tags efficiently.

6

Denormalization Use Cases

This chapter might well be the most important one in this book. Why? That's because it deals with the most common design use cases: storing objects and the relationships between them. In this chapter, we are going to discuss the following topics:

- Storing all the objects for a user
- A popularity contest using counters
- Storing tags efficiently

These three areas represent the most common design patterns in the following manner. *Users* is one of the most popular words in the life of designers, start-ups, and established companies. They are people for whom we do all the work, and they are a measure of our success. So, we need to store their information properly, and this is what the topic *Storing all the objects for a user* covers.

Popularity contests occur very often in life. So, our software needs to be optimized for this. Which is the most popular movie, who is the most popular actor, which food is trending at a restaurant, and so on. The picture shown next illustrates exactly this; the popularity contests between movies with numbers, which being in millions of dollars explain why such contests are considered important by many.

Tags and tag clouds have been the novelty for the past few years. Attention spans have decreased further, and people look for easier ways to summarize information. This is where tags come in, generated by the user who creates the content or automatically. In any case, we need to store them efficiently and retrieve them quickly. How can you do this? This will be explained in the chapter.

This chapter is also very interactive and educational. Time and again, you will be presented with challenges, allowed to think about it and to offer your solution, and then compare the solution with the one offered in this book.

Lest you think that the problem of attention span is something new, here is a quote from Jerome K's book, *The Diary of a Pilgrimage*, published in 1891:

> *I have purposely put the matter in a light and attractive form, so that I may secure the attention of the young and the frivolous. I do not want them to notice, as they go on, that they are being instructed; and I have, therefore, endeavored to disguise from them, so far as is practicable, that this is either an exceptionally clever or an exceptionally useful work. I want to do them good without their knowing it. I want to do you all good — to improve your minds and to make you think, if I can.*

> *What you will think after you have read the book, I do not want to know; indeed, I would rather not know. It will be sufficient reward for me to feel that I have done my duty, and to receive a percentage on the gross sales.*

The following picture shows what a young artist imagines a movie popularity contest to be, the one for which we will be designing our HBase:

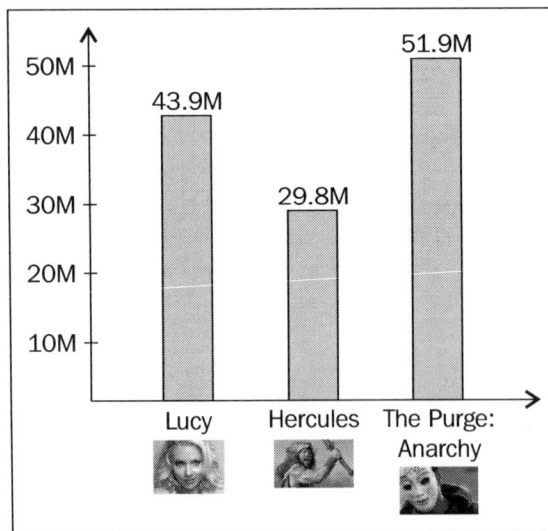

To get the most out of this chapter, we encourage you to treat it as a design exercise. When presented with a problem, don't rush to read the answer. Rather, close the book and work on your own design solution. Then, our solution will be much more interesting for you, as you will be able to see where your solution is better, if it is, and learn from ours, if you see fit.

Storing all the objects for a user

We have already discussed the user table concept in *Chapter 3, Using HBase Tables for Single Entities*. Let's review this, because we are going to build upon it.

You are building a website for video upload and viewing. The first thing that you would like to do is store information about your users. What would you want to know about your users? This time, please close the book and try to design your table, unlike in *Chapter 3, Using HBase Tables for Single Entities*. Here is what you would want to store:

- Username
- First name, last name, and any other personal information you want
- Password (encrypted in real life)
- One or more e-mails
- Other usability items

This is how a reasonable answer will look:

```
CREATE TABLE users (
    username varchar,
    firstname varchar,
    lastname varchar,
    email list<varchar>,
    password varchar,
    created_date timestamp,
    PRIMARY KEY (username)
);
```

Note that, as shown in *Chapter 3, Using HBase Tables for Single Entities*, you don't need to generate an ID, because the username is a good identifier and it is unique. That's nice! No more sequence generators for you; you don't need them. As far as making usernames unique is concerned, we have already discussed this in *Chapter 3, Using HBase Tables for Single Entities*.

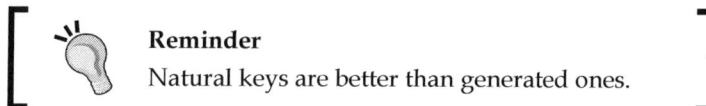

> **Reminder**
> Natural keys are better than generated ones.

Of course, you want to save their e-mail IDs, don't you? Don't store them elsewhere and use a join! It will be very inefficient. When there is user interaction and the user profile changes, you don't want to update all the contacts in other tables. Moreover, if you store the e-mail IDs in the same table, you also get a row-level isolation for the cases where you are updating a profile and another process is also updating it. If e-mail IDs are stored in a separate table, this might be harder due to the distributed mode.

When storing a group of e-mail IDs, a list is a better fit than a set. Why? The e-mail IDs are ordered by how you insert them. You can control this order. Thus, for example, it has a record of the primary e-mail. A set will not work for this. However, the primary advantage of a list is that you don't need fields, such as `email1`, `email2`, or `email3`.

Dealing with lost usernames and passwords

Now imagine that a user has lost his/her username, but the user remembers his/her e-mail ID. You just keyed everything on the username, so without it we are lost. You can read *all* the entries in the database in the attempt of finding this e-mail ID. However, I don't have to convince you how bad this approach is.

So, I challenge you to design your approach. Most of my students, when presented with this challenge in class, started changing the basic `user` table, preparing it for additional queries. However, the right approach is more radical. Here's some advice from one of the leading NoSQL architects, Patrick McFadin:

> *"Good question! (We are not alone in our struggle)."*

I mention this topic in other venues, too. What do you do if you want to look up by e-mail ID? This might be a good place for an index table, as follows:

```
create table email_index (
  domain text,
  username text,
  user_id text,
  PRIMARY KEY (domain, username)
);
```

So, with an address such as patrick@datastax.com, you will create this insert:

```
insert into email_index (domain,username,user_id) values
('datastax.com', 'patrick','pmcfadin');
```

```
select user_id from email_index where domain='datastax.com' and
username='patrick';
```

On large domains, such as gmail.com, you might want to expand the domain part of the include part of the username. It will give you more manageable partitions.

We saw what Patrick does. The essential points here are:

- Create another table to answer your queries. Nothing is available in NoSQL for efficient secondary indices; so do it yourself.

- Denormalize. That is really the key. If you need to, store the same data twice or more times, as long as you can get efficient queries to get your answers fast. It is true that your code needs to take care of updating the same information in other tables as well, yet the performance benefits are paramount.

- Think about efficiency when you are designing.

Why do we divide the e-mail IDs by domains? The answer is efficiency. Notice that we don't want to have too small or too large partitions, but we want them balanced. Is this for performance reasons? What are the arguments against tall and narrow rows?

These are called **index** tables or **lookup** tables. This is a perfectly valid way of building up fast data models and are used pretty heavily in the production environment.

The number of cells is a performance consideration. Even though theoretically you can store 2 billion cells per row, there are trade-offs in the speed at which you can access them. Patrick found that tens of thousands of cells is an upper limit before you start eating into 95 percentiles of your read latencies—mostly due to deserialization costs on the larger indexes.

So, just to make sure, we have a question—why not have absolutely thin and tall tables with one value per key? Will this be inefficient?

The answer is that it is mostly inefficient. Lots of rows can cause cache hit problems and huge bloom filters.

Generating data for performance testing

There are many rules for testing, and I am offering you my set of rules here. My ideas on this come from the now classic book by Scott Meyers, *Effective C++*, where Scott gives you the three rules of performance optimization; that is, a) don't do it, b) don't do it, c) and do it only after profiling.

The same applies to performance testing on big data. Never take anything for granted. Dispute every conclusion and require it to be verified by testing. In our case, the best way to confirm all the performance considerations we just stated categorically is to generate a sufficient amount of data and perform the actual tests ourselves.

As we already mentioned in *Chapter 3, Using HBase Tables for Single Entities*, our lab code on the Web provides you with sufficient opportunity to do so. Here are the instructions:

- Clone or download this project on GitHub (`https://github.com/markkerzner/hbase-book`). It contains compiled JAR files, so all that you need to run it is Java.

- In the **generators** lab, run this generator:

```
cd generators
./run_generate_users.sh 100 10
```

- Then, you can load the generated user data.

Tables for storing videos

You, the reader, need to add an `entity` table that will store many videos for a unique user. Please close the book and design this table.

If you have not stored the video in this table, you did the right thing. This shows that you have been reading attentively and absorbing the material so far. Let's recapitulate why you should not do it:

- A video is not a part of the `videos` table. It might be ready when the video is not.

- If you combine the big and small data pieces, performance tuning will be messed up and your debugging and optimization will be rendered useless.

- Besides, a video is usually stored in a content delivery system.

Here's our solution:

```
//  Entity table that will store many videos for a unique user
CREATE TABLE videos (
    videoid uuid,
    videoname varchar,
    username varchar,
    description varchar,
    // need-to-have
    // location map<varchar,varchar>,
    // instead using List
    location List <varchar>, // compound key
    tags List<varchar>,
    upload_date timestamp,
    PRIMARY KEY (videoid)
);
```

The points to note here are:

- UUID is a first-class citizen. We told you not to sequence, but that's only when it is autogenerated. UUIDs on the other hand are OK. In fact, the video name is not a natural ID.

- A username belongs to one user, but note that we duplicated the username that we needed right here right now.

- A set is not a list, but it's exactly what we need here. Unfortunately, Phoenix does not provide for a set object, so we use a list. However, keep in mind the real data structure that we need.

- Note that we made the location a `<String, String>` map, where the key is the location and the value is the URI of the video. That's because content delivery systems usually store videos in different locations. In this way, we are again imitating lists.

Manual exercises

To manually insert a video row, you need to do this:

```
INSERT INTO videos
(videoid, videoname, username, description, location, tags, upload_date)
VALUES
(18134b9d-6222-4f0e-b06d-4ba1e6c62f50, 'my cat', 'johnsmith', 'this is
my cat', {'us' : 'http://right.here'}, {'cats', 'pets'}, '2013-09-09
21:33:15');
```

Phoenix can be used to generate the UUID; the one that we used here was generated with Java code.

Generating data for performance testing

Similar to the code we just saw, in order to generate data for performance testing, clone or download this project on GitHub (`https://github.com/markkerzner/hbase-book`). It contains compiled JAR files, so all that you need to run it is Java.

In the generators lab, run this generator:

```
cd generators
./run_generate_videos.sh 100 10
```

Then, you can load the generated user data with this statement. Use a preload for HBase, described in a later chapter of this book.

To analyze the SQL query, examine the `videos.txt` file.

What about performance? We are using lists. They are serialized, and this incurs a performance cost. Generate data with 10 locations or with 100 locations. Run it to find out the size at which the performance of this location object becomes a problem.

Now, you can run the inserts by copying and pasting the generated video's data.

Run it with 5, 10, 20, or other locations. When does the performance noticeably deteriorate? Try to find this experimentally on your own and then visit our repository to view our results.

The points to make a note of here are:

- Never optimize before you run profiling
- Is tracing available in Phoenix?

Here's the answer that I got from Jesse Yates. Keep in mind that this was true at the time of writing this book and the situation will most likely be further along at the time of your reading the book.

As Jesse said, "I worked on adding tracing into Phoenix, but never finished it up; it would use Cloudera's **HTrace** library since that is already bundled into HBase 0.96 and higher versions. With the 4.0 Phoenix branch (which is based on HBase 0.96 and higher versions), this integration should be even easier, and might actually get finished!"

Until then, you can explain this as follows:

The URL `https://github.com/jyates/phoenix/tree/tracing` worked at the time of Hadoop 2, but never quite brought it the extra mile necessary to roll it into Phoenix properly. Interestingly, it has also been the main reason why I made the build multimodule (and included the Hadoop Compatibility stuff).

So, there is little doubt that tracing is available. We can also expect it to be available with the Java API, and this is how you can approach measuring performance in production, by writing a custom load testing code.

Please keep in mind that tracing has its own overhead, so use it only for debugging and profiling and not for overall performance measurements.

As an advanced exercise, solve this:

What will you use to fix the performance problem of having too many maps?

> **Hint**
> Use another table to index locations. Share this solution on the book's forum.

A popularity contest

Imagine you need to record the popularity of videos. If someone gives a rating, this increases the total number of ratings and the exact rating that the user gave goes towards calculating the average rating of the video. How will you design a table for this?

Please close the book and try to design your solution.

OK, now that you have your solution, let's take a look at ours:

```
CREATE TABLE video_rating (
    videoid uuid,
    rating_counter counter,
    rating_total counter,
    PRIMARY KEY (videoid)
);
```

Here are the rules for the ratings:

- The rating counter is incremented when someone gives any rating. We will use the example of three stars as a rating value.
- A rating total is a cumulative record of the rating, so for the three stars rating, you give ++3 for the counter.
- The average is calculated as `rating_total/rating_counter`.

You might have also come up with not-so-perfect solutions. Here are some of the possibly wrong solutions:

- **Read the number and increment it**: This is an antipattern, so it reads before performing the writes (this leads to concurrency problems in a distributed environment).
- **Store every rating and sum them up later**: This is incorrect, because you need to design with queries in mind, not with the data in mind. If you store the sum, you can use it for the query. If you store each rating, you need to calculate it for the query.

Once you have designed your table for ratings, do this exercise:

Write a SQL statement that will add a rating of three stars for a given video.

A solution for this is given here.

Note that you don't have to prefill the table with any data. Rather, you can start using a new table for updates right away. That is the property of counters:

```
UPDATE video_rating SET rating_counter = rating_counter + 1,
rating_total = rating_total + 3  WHERE
videoid = 58178e0a-5ea1-4b65-8bb8-a3f610b5cf68;
```

Now, verify the rating by querying the table.

The section tag index

Let's describe just one more tagging technique. Let's say you need to place tags on the videos. For example, you might need to find all the videos for a given tag. What might be a wrong thing to do is to go through the `videos` table looking for this tag. Don't iterate through all the videos looking for the tags. So, how do you do that?

Try this exercise.

How will you solve the requirement for a tag functionality? Do it yourself first and then go back and compare it with our answer.

A solution for this is to create a `tag_index` table, as follows:

```
CREATE TABLE tag_index (
    tag varchar,
    videoid uuid,
    timestamp timestamp,
    PRIMARY KEY (tag, videoid)
);
```

The points to make a note of here are:

- We are not storing a list or a set of videos, as it will be a wrong RDBMS pattern. Can you explain why?
- We get very fast writes.
- We get reasonably fast reads because it is a slice operation (essentially, it is a group by operation).

Try the following exercise:

Write a query to get all the videos for a given tag. Check our GitHub repository for the answers.

Here's one bonus exercise for you: what if you want to tag videos by popularity? Search for the answer, and publish a good solution on the book's forum.

Summary

In this chapter, we learned important NoSQL and HBase design principles, that is, consistent denormalization and creation of new (index) tables any time we were presented with an additional query. That's the rule—define the queries first and then design the tables to answer these queries efficiently. If you can't answer a query with the current table structure, you might be faced with a dilemma of having queries that will run quite slow or have the additional burden of maintaining index tables.

In the next chapter, we will conclude our journey of the advanced NoSQL design principles, that is, many-to-many relationships, time-related events (not to be confused with time series data), and dealing with transactions in NoSQL (where I need to remind you that transactions are not provided).

7
Advanced Patterns for Data Modeling

In this chapter, we will continue with the fun and educational games that we started in the previous chapter. I will present you with a problem, challenge you to solve it, and then show you the solution that I have garnered from experience and by learning from experts. Feel free to challenge my solution and come up with a better one. As one sage has said, "Much have I learned from my teachers, more from my colleagues, but most from my students."

Therefore, go to www.hbasedesignpatterns.com and leave your solutions there.

Meanwhile, here are the topics that we will tackle in this chapter:

- Many-to-many relationships in HBase's event time data (keeping track of what is going on)
- Dealing with transactions

So, let's start.

HOW TO CREATE A STABLE DATA MODEL

This picture illustrates an artist's view of us approaching the data modeling problems in HBase. At times, it might be overwhelming, so our characters have gone with the most general approach of something leads to something.

Many-to-many relationships in HBase

We have said many times that HBase does not have the regular SQL model. Thus, it has no indexes and no joins. So, how do you maintain many-to-many relationships that are so common in the world? Let me give you an example.

In the problem involving students and courses in the previous chapter, we had many students that could be taking a course, but we could also have many courses that a student could be taking.

We will approach this problem as follows. First, I will give you a few schematic examples to illustrate the most important parts of the approach. Second, we will take a look at an industrial-strength solution, using a video site as an example.

Creating a many-to-many relationship for a university with students and courses

Imagine that you are modeling data for a large college or university. Coursera (www.coursera.com) might be a good example of a large college; their courses collect between 100,000 to 300,000 students, and incidentally, they are also an example of unbelievable analytics capabilities.

So, in this world university, you have students and you have courses. One student can take many courses, and one course can be taken by many students. This is a typical many-to-many relationship.

Putting this a bit more formally, here's the problem that you need to solve:

- Students
  - Student_id
  - Name
  - Email
- Course
  - Course_id
  - Name
  - Teacher
- A student can take many courses
- A course can be taken by many students
- Queries
  - Find all courses taken by a student
  - Find all students enrolled in a course

Design an Hbase table/schema for the following real-world example.

We all know that the classical approach in the SQL world would be to put all the students in one table and all the courses in another and to have a join table, named appropriately as STUDENT_COURSE, which will indicate their relationship. However, as discussed in *Chapter 6*, *Denormalization Use Cases*, it is preferable to avoid joins in big data, since they are very expensive computationally.

The timer signifies that you need to close the book now and think about the approaches that you can take, perhaps sketch them. Team competition works great, and if you are a teacher, you can assign this problem to teams of students.

Now that you are back, let's take a look at our proposed solution:

info			courses	
student_id	Name	email	course_id1	course_id2

courses	info		students	
course_id	Name	Teacher	student_id1	Student_id2

You can now see what we have done. We have denormalized the data and stored each element twice. The first table lists all the courses for a given student in one row. The second table lists all the students for a given course, also in one row. Thus, the same student-course relationship is stored twice in our schema. It is true that you will have to provide double the amount of storage volume. However, hard drive space is cheap. Also, it is true that your code logic will have to maintain two tables. However, what you get in return is a no-limit scalability, and this is the name of the game nowadays.

Let's take a look at some of the technical aspects of this design:

- The student-course relationship is represented as columns:

  Remember, column names can be dynamic. This means that you can store as many courses as you want and can call these columns anything you like. Thus, you can get all the courses for a student in one read, without an expensive join, which would otherwise become a bottleneck.

  Here's a question for you: how do you write a query to find out whether a student is taking a course? Again, please think of an answer first.

  Here's our query that can do this for you:

  Examine the value of `Students` `[student_id]` `[courses]` `[course_id]`.

  As an exercise, create such a table in the HBase shell and store/retrieve some values. Check the book's repository on GitHub for our solution.

- The student-course relationship is represented in both the tables:

  Note that we have denormalized both the tables. As you can see, it is a common approach; if I need a relationship and HBase does not provide it out of the box, I will just create another table to model this relationship.

You might also ask what is stored in the values in this table? This is illustrated in the following diagram:

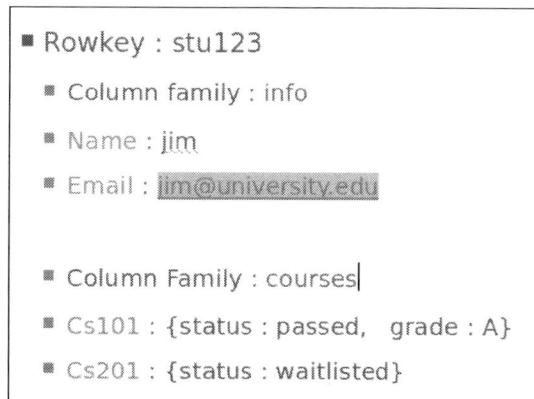

- Rowkey : stu123
  - Column family : info
  - Name : jim
  - Email : jim@university.edu

  - Column Family : courses
  - Cs101 : {status : passed,   grade : A}
  - Cs201 : {status : waitlisted}

Imagine that you need to store and retrieve all the comments for a video. However, remember that you will also need all the comments for a given user as well.

Creating a many-to-many relationship for a social network

Imagine that you are creating a social network. OK, you might not have the whole world on it, but you might come up with a specific interest group. So, you can imagine a group of all Haiku lovers who also appreciate a good drink. Here's your problem:

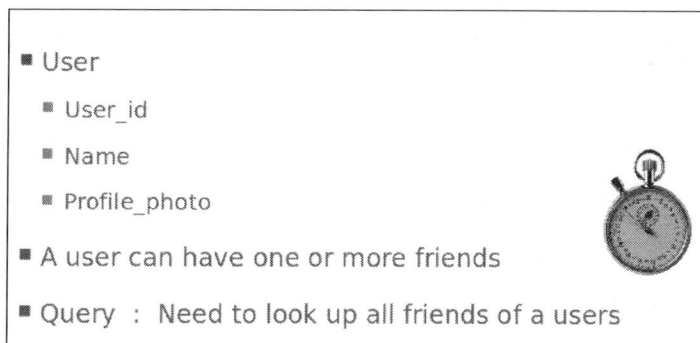

- User
  - User_id
  - Name
  - Profile_photo
- A user can have one or more friends
- Query : Need to look up all friends of a users

Again, the timer shows that you should close the book and design your tables. Nothing teaches as well as practice. Let me illustrate this with a story. The sages of old debated for 18 months: which is more important, the study or the deed? Having exhausted all philosophical arguments, they resorted to voting, and the school which was more numerous won, "Study is more important, because it leads to the deed."

In our context, immediately after studying the theory of the NoSQL design, you need to apply it in practice. Here's our answer to this problem:

users	info	friends
<user_id>	Username Email Profile_photo	<user_id>:type <user_id>:type

Let's discuss this:

- Friendship is represented in columns:

    We will have to update anyone's information at two places, that is, in the <user_id> and friends columns, especially if we store more information about the users than we show in this simple sketch of the implementation. That's all right; the columns that are stored in HBase are sorted, so finding a particular user in the friends list is fast.

- When user A is friends with user B, how many entries will be created?

    The answer is two. Friendship is mutual; thus, if user B is a friend of user A, then user A is a friend of user B. We will write two records, one for user A and one for user B. Again, this is fast enough. Since we are essentially writing <user_id> and <friend_id> in the <user_id> row, each write goes independently into its column. In the physical implementation of HBase, this can be executed in parallel. The code does not need to read all the columns for the <user_id> row before it updates the row—this is the beauty of NoSQL.

- What happens when a user account is deleted?

    Again, you will have to update two rows, one for user A and his/her friend (user B), and one for user B and his/her friend (user A). The physical implementation of the deletion in HBase is writing a tombstone marker, which leads to no row lock and is fast.

As a practical matter, most systems today probably don't delete users outright but put them in the *deleted* state instead. This does not change our design.

The danger here is of unknown friends. If you don't perform the `<user_id>` deletion correctly, you might have friends that were deleted and which might show up as unknown.

With this preparatory work, we are ready for the problem of the day, also called *soup du jour* in French. If you got this joke, then what does *soup du siecle* mean? With this out of the way, we are ready to start with the promised video site based on a real-world problem.

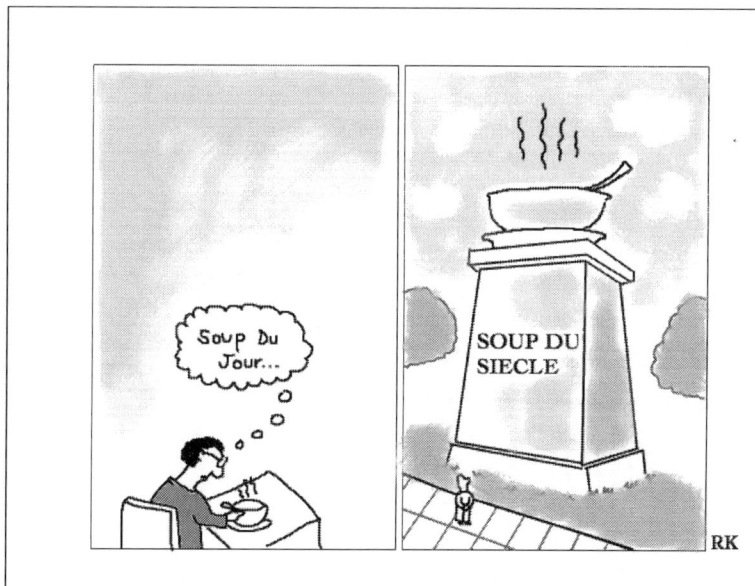

Applying the many-to-many relationship techniques for a video site

The problem of a many-to-many relationship is a common one, in HBase and in Cassandra as well as in many NoSQL databases. It is true that some NoSQL databases give you limited secondary indices, but this is as far as it goes—they impose a performance penalty and are not generic. So, you are on your own. However, we have already dealt with this in the example before, and we know that we need to introduce additional tables to implement this functionality for us.

So, here is a real-world problem that will allow you to showcase your NoSQL modeling skills to the fullest. If you are teaching, you can make this a graduation project.

Imagine that you need to store and retrieve all the comments for a video. However, remember that you will also need all the comments for a given user.

Think about a design for this problem and then come back to take a look at our proposed answer.

Here's our answer to this problem.

We will need two index tables, as follows:

```
// Comments as a many-to-many
// Looking from the video side to many users
CREATE TABLE comments_by_video (
    videoid uuid,
    username varchar,
    comment_ts timestamp,
    comment varchar,
    PRIMARY KEY (videoid,comment_ts,username)
) WITH CLUSTERING ORDER BY (comment_ts DESC, username ASC);


// looking from the user side to many videos
CREATE TABLE comments_by_user (
    username varchar,
    videoid uuid,
    comment_ts timestamp,
    comment varchar,
    PRIMARY KEY (username,comment_ts,videoid)
) WITH CLUSTERING ORDER BY (comment_ts DESC, videoid ASC);
```

This should create an *Aha!* moment, where a light bulb comes up (if it did not come up before), and you might heave a sigh of satisfaction.

Now, let's solidify this in a lab.

To generate input data, run the following script:

```
./generate_comment_indices.sh 5 10
```

If you want to find out the meaning of each of the parameters, run the script without the parameters to get the help screen.

To import the data, use the following command:

```
cqlsh (use HBase import) -f generated/comments_by_users.txt
```

Now, let's think about performance. What happens when you have a controversial video with 1,000,000 comments per video? When does the performance suffer? Can you find this parameter? At what size does our design break and require an enhancement? What should this enhancement be?

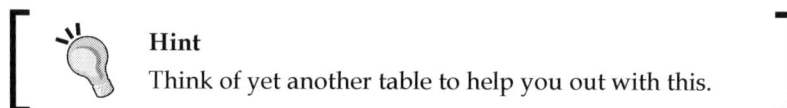

> **Hint**
> Think of yet another table to help you out with this.

Event time data – keeping track of what is going on

In this lab, we will track events and also illustrate a compound key.

Imagine that you need to track what's going on. Our user watches the video and then goes to a full screen with a different player. Then, he/she leaves from home, jumps into a car, and his/her dad takes him/her to the school, while he/she resumes watching the video. We need to track such events. For simplicity, we will consider our event as consisting of start, stop, and pause. (Later, you can enhance this with user-specific events.)

Here are the questions you need to consider and be able to answer in your design from your user's point of view:

- When is the last time I stopped the event?
- When is the last time I started the event?
- What is the last thing that happened?
- How many times did I start the event?

Follow the lab given here.

Reader, persevere! This is the last time you need to close the book and come up with your own solution. After you design your solution, reopen the book and take a look at the answer.

Our proposed answer is as follows:

```
// Time series wide row with reverse comparator
CREATE TABLE video_event (
    videoid uuid,
    username varchar,
    event varchar,
    event_timestamp timeuuid,
    video_timestamp bigint,
    PRIMARY KEY ((videoid,username), event_timestamp,event)
) WITH CLUSTERING ORDER BY (event_timestamp DESC,event ASC);
```

Again, let's play with the data, so that we get a feel of what's going on.

To generate the data for your testing, run the following script in the book's code (please refer to our repository for instructions on how to run this script):

```
./generate_video_events.sh 5 10
```

Then, import the data into HBase using Phoenix.

The following is the sample data content that you might see:

videoid	username	event_timestamp	event	video_timestamp
ecefa72b-a27b-4cdb-ab5c-9e37fc4d4838	sdamn	aa51ef80-2598-11e3-a417-14109fe64b55	PAUSE	8214860286272927769
8ae51b79-985d-4788-813e-1dd99f97291a	lcinhk	2398ccc0-2598-11e3-a787-22000ab20a62	PAUSE	7292542489339765911
81987c60-aedd-4106-8ed2-5ac90ba4af48	gxoudtml	2399b720-2598-11e3-a787-22000ab20a62	START	5270741755532525812
dbc43273-87d0-441e-811b-8a1b8fc4630f	wajmvdamnts	23979440-2598-11e3-a787-22000ab20a62	PAUSE	8791000015007995090
92b9e9a7-20ca-4871-baa8-952ff52f1640	rqrmszc	aa521690-2598-11e3-a417-14109fe64b55	START	3182197244260450299
cda2edba-d104-4436-98e0-543b45e1be45	brcvlxfkrqbx	0f60c130-2599-11e3-a4fa-14109fe64b55	STOP	4930183707336446788
60523059-9e0f-4c47-bf0b-9b427e982fd4	xotwnbs	ad6e8e40-2597-11e3-aa83-14109fe64b55	START	1010157598432526383
bcf703ba-d690-4ab0-8026-539fc852fd88	xdnclwunryybt	23983080-2598-11e3-a787-22000ab20a62	RESUME	8715428483392586360
a92978e8-a44f-4323-ae7d-f67d2e97e6a5	wnxgvt	0f609a20-2599-11e3-a4fa-14109fe64b55	STOP	8938507249456401093
bead4c6f-45ff-43b4-b163-c5e4d4a759bf	qwmqpn	23985790-2598-11e3-a787-22000ab20a62	PAUSE	2889794325790967408

Now that you have designed the solution and run the lab with the actual data, here are the points to be noted for this design:

- `video_timestamp` is not part of the row key. Therefore, all `video_timestamp` entries go into the same row, in effect forming a wide row, where you can get all the events for a given video and user in one query.

- Can you determine the size of the table at which the performance deteriorates?

- Our solution will be very slow for large table sizes, so what is your proposed solution?

Here are some advanced questions that we want you to ponder on; also, you can share your answers on the book's site:

- Can you determine how many people never finish watching a particular video?

- With this, here's an analytics question. What is the problem with that video? What videos are never watched to completion? Why?

These are really advanced, real-life questions. Try to find a solution for the problems we just mentioned. The hint here is to create yet another table for the last five videos that you watched, as follows:

```
CREATE TABLE video_playlist (
        username varchar.
        play_ts timestamp;
        videoid uuid
        PRIMARY KEY (username,play_ts)
) WITH CLUSTERING ORDER BY (play_ts DESC);
```

This is another table to maintain, but this will provide you with an answer in a reasonable time.

Dealing with transactions

How do you implement transactions? What a question! You might say, "My SQL database provides them for me!" Indeed, in your code, you start a transaction, lock the database row or two rows, and either complete the transaction or roll it back.

However, it is not as easy as it sounds. Even in the world of SQL, this leads to two-phase commits, and they in turn lead to locks to the database; hence, the application remains unavailable for a period of time. However, if you are a bank, you really have no choice. People won't like it if their money goes out of their account (the transaction starts) occasionally and then due to a malfunctioning of the system that does not have transactions, this money does not end up either with their friend they've been sending the money to or in their other account. A bank must have transactions. However, most of us don't have this.

We have lived happily without transactions, thus accepting occasional failures. In the classic paper *Your Coffee Shop Doesn't Use Two-Phase Commit* at `http://www.eaipatterns.com/docs/IEEE_Software_Design_2PC.pdf`, Gregor Hohpe described the operation of asynchronous processing, which accounts for failures with occasional losses (spilled drinks) and is different from the transaction of the you-at-the-bank-teller relationship. This shows that we can use systems that are not strictly deterministic as long as they give satisfactory results, more or less.

Another example would be if you are buying a book on Amazon and discover that at the end of the checkout, somebody has already snatched the last copy. Pechal'ka, as the Russians would say, "A little sorrow."

All right, so having determined the parameters under which we can accept an approximation rather than a genuine transaction, how do we implement it? The answer is you can do it yourself. Here are the possible approaches:

- Model your transaction around a row:

  We know that updates to a row in a column family are atomic. Therefore, you can model your data in such a way that the transaction affects only one row and you only need to update a single row in a single CF at once. Thus, you turn around and model your data around transactions, rather than the other way around. Admittedly, this is tricky, but it can certainly be done in some situations.

- Model multiple rows around one locking row:

  If you are only dealing with multiple row inserts (and not updates), you can have one of the rows act as a commit by essentially validating the presence of the other rows. For example, say you were performing an operation where you wanted to create an account row and five user rows at once (this is an unlikely example, but bear with me). You can insert five rows into the users' CF and then add one row into the accounts CF, which acts as the commit. If something went wrong before the account could be created, users that have been created so far would be orphaned and become unusable, as your business logic can ensure that they can't exist without an account. You could also have an offline cleanup process that sweeps away orphans.

Try to model your updates as idempotent column inserts instead. How do you model updates as inserts? Instead of munging the value directly, you can insert a column containing the operation you want to perform (for example, add 5). It will work like the *Consistent Vote Counting in Cassandra* implementation, found at `https://gist.github.com/416666`. How do you make the inserts idempotent? Make sure that the column names correspond to a request ID or some other identifier that will be identical across redrives of a given (perhaps, originally failed) request. This can leave your datastore in a temporarily inconsistent state but will eventually become consistent after a successful redrive of the original request.

- Another approach is to take a snapshot of all the original values that you're about to munge somewhere else (in this case, ZooKeeper), make your updates, and then delete the snapshot (this delete needs to be atomic). If the snapshot data is not deleted, then subsequent accessors (even readers) of the data rows need to do the rollback of the previous transaction themselves before they can read/write this data. They do the rollback just by overwriting the current values with what is in the snapshot. It offloads the work of the rollback to the next worker that accesses the data. This approach probably needs a generic or high-level programming layer to handle all the details and complexity, and it doesn't seem like it was ever added to cages.

When elucidating the transactions in the NoSQL world, the authors gratefully acknowledge their debt to John Laban, Jérémy Sevellec, Dominic Williams, and DataStax experts, who provided these in the form of answers on NoSQL forums.

We are currently working on additional code examples for implementing transactions in NoSQL, so expect to find these in the book's GitHub repository at `https://github.com/elephantscale/hbase-book` as well as discussions on `http://hbasedesignpatterns.com`.

Trafodion – transactional SQL on HBase

The latest development in the world of transactions for HBase is **Trafodion**. It claims to fill the missing gap in the Hadoop infrastructure, that is, transactions. More specifically, it offers the following:

- Fully functional ANSI SQL language support
- JDBC/ODBC connectivity for Linux/Windows clients
- ACID distributed transaction protection across multiple statements, tables, and rows
- Support for large data sets using a parallel-aware query optimizer

Thus, it presents a major competitor to the Phoenix driver and an aspiration to Google's large transactional database called **Spanner**, which is not yet available as open source. In the early stages of adoption, at the time when this book goes to print, Trafodion might nevertheless be a game changer, and we plan to provide the examples of its use in our repository as well as write about it on the book's site at www.hbasedesignpatterns.com.

Summary

In this chapter, we looked at very advanced real-world design problems in the NoSQL world, with HBase as a solution platform. We saw the common patterns, and with this, we are ready to tackle most of the NoSQL/HBase projects.

We thus leave the highfalutin world of NoSQL design. In the words of Shakespeare, "Thus have I, Wall, my part discharged so; And, being done, thus Wall away doth go."

In the next chapter, we will address another kind of real-word problem, HBase performance and monitoring.

Performance Optimization

8

In the previous chapter, you learned some of the approaches to advanced modeling techniques for HBase. In this chapter, we will talk about how to write high performance and scalable HBase applications.

In particular, will take a look at the following topics:

- The bulk loading of data into HBase
- Profiling HBase applications
- Tips to get good performance on writes
- Tips to get good performance on reads
- Benchmarking and load testing HBase

Loading bulk data into HBase

When deploying HBase for the first time, we usually need to import a significant amount of data. This is called **initial loading** or **bootstrapping**. There are three methods that can be used to import data into HBase, given as follows:

- Using the Java API to insert data into HBase. This can be done in a single client, using single or multiple threads.

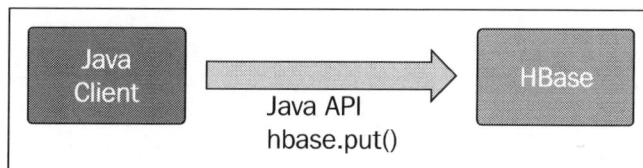

- Using MapReduce to insert data in parallel (this approach also uses the Java API), as shown in the following diagram:

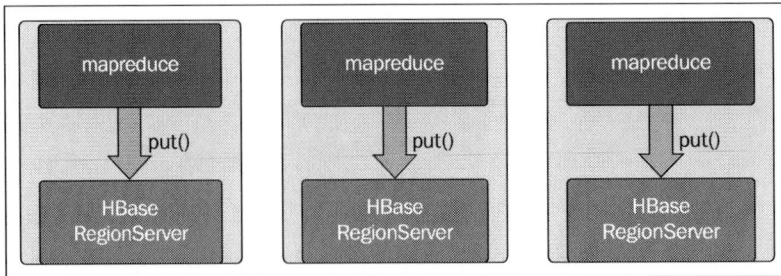

- Using MapReduce to generate HBase store files in parallel in bulk and then import them into HBase directly. (This approach does not require the use of the API; it does not require code and is very efficient.)

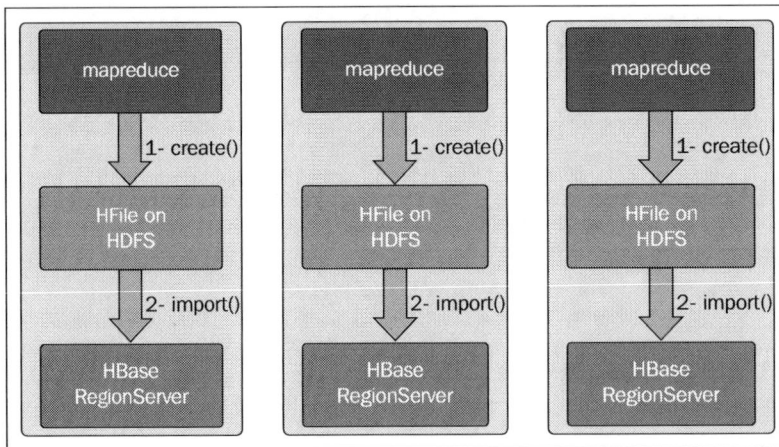

On comparing the three methods speed wise, we have the following order:

Java client < MapReduce insert < HBase file import

The Java client and MapReduce use HBase APIs to insert data. MapReduce runs on multiple machines and can exploit parallelism. However, both of these methods go through the write path in HBase.

Importing HBase files directly, however, skips the usual write path. HBase files already have data in the correct format that HBase understands. That's why importing them is much faster than using MapReduce and the Java client.

We covered the Java API earlier. Let's start with how to insert data using MapReduce.

Importing data into HBase using MapReduce

MapReduce is the distributed processing engine of Hadoop. Usually, programs read/write data from HDFS. Luckily, HBase supports MapReduce. HBase can be the **source** and the **sink** for MapReduce programs. A source means MapReduce programs can read from HBase, and sink means results from MapReduce can be sent to HBase.

The following diagram illustrates various sources and sinks for MapReduce:

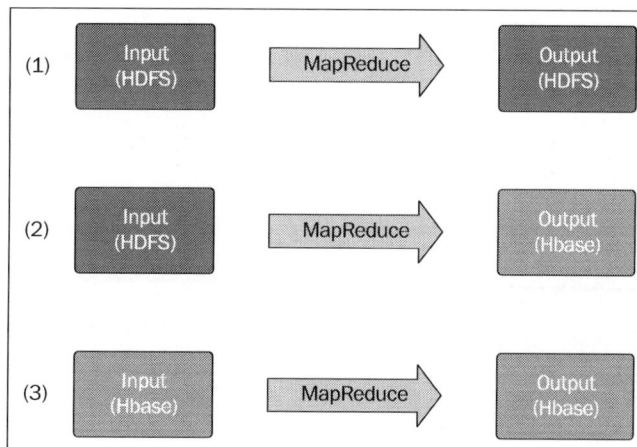

The diagram we just saw can be summarized as follows:

Scenario	Source	Sink	Description
1	HDFS	HDFS	This is a typical MapReduce method that reads data from HDFS and also sends the results to HDFS.
2	HDFS	HBase	This imports the data from HDFS into HBase. It's a very common method that is used to import data into HBase for the first time.
3	HBase	HBase	Data is read from HBase and written to it. It is most likely that these will be two separate HBase clusters. It's usually used for backups and mirroring.

Importing data from HDFS into HBase

Let's say we have lots of data in HDFS and want to import it into HBase. We are going to write a MapReduce program that reads from HDFS and inserts data into HBase. This is depicted in the second scenario in the table we just saw.

Now, we'll be setting up the environment for the following discussion. We presume that you have already set up HBase through the Kiji distribution or are using any other approach described in *Chapter 1, Starting Out with HBase*. In addition, you can find the code and the data for this discussion in our GitHub repository at `https://github.com/elephantscale/hbase-book`.

The dataset we will use is the sensor data. Our (imaginary) sensor data is stored in HDFS as CSV (comma-separated values) text files. This is how their format looks:

```
Sensor_id, max temperature, min temperature
```

Here is some sample data:

- `sensor11,90,70`
- `sensor22,80,70`
- `sensor31,85,72`
- `sensor33,75,72`

We have two sample files (`sensor-data1.csv` and `sensor-data2.csv`) in our repository under the `/data` directory. Feel free to inspect them.

The first thing we have to do is copy these files into HDFS.

Create a directory in HDFS as follows:

```
$   hdfs   dfs  -mkdir   hbase-import
```

Now, copy the files into HDFS:

```
$   hdfs   dfs   -put   sensor-data*   hbase-import/
```

Verify that the files exist as follows:

```
$   hdfs   dfs   -ls   hbase-import
```

We are ready to insert this data into HBase. Note that we are designing the table to match the CSV files we are loading for ease of use.

Our row key is `sensor_id`.

We have one column family and we call it f (short for family).

Now, we will store two columns, max temperature and min temperature, in this column family.

Pig for MapReduce

Pig allows you to write MapReduce programs at a very high level, and inserting data into HBase is just as easy.

Here's a Pig script that reads the sensor data from HDFS and writes it in HBase:

```
-- ## hdfs-to-hbase.pig
data = LOAD 'hbase-import/' using PigStorage(',') as (sensor_
id:chararray, max:int, min:int);
-- describe data;
-- dump data;
```

Now, store the data in hbase://sensors using the following line of code:

```
org.apache.pig.backend.hadoop.hbase.HBaseStorage('f:max,f:min');
```

After creating the table, in the first command, we will load data from the hbase-import directory in HDFS.

The schema for the data is defined as follows:

```
Sensor_id  : chararray (string)
max : int
min : int
```

The describe and dump statements can be used to inspect the data; in Pig, describe will give you the structure of the data object you have, and dump will output all the data to the terminal.

The final STORE command is the one that inserts the data into HBase. Let's analyze how it is structured:

- INTO 'hbase://sensors': This tells Pig to connect to the sensors HBase table.

- org.apache.pig.backend.hadoop.hbase.HBaseStorage: This is the Pig class that will be used to write in HBase. Pig has adapters for multiple data stores.

- The first field in the tuple, sensor_id, will be used as a row key.

- We are specifying the column names for the `max` and `min` fields (`f:max` and `f:min`, respectively). Note that we have to specify the column family (`f:`) to qualify the columns.

Before running this script, we need to create an HBase table called `sensors`. We can do this from the HBase shell, as follows:

```
$  hbase shell
$  create 'sensors' ,  'f'
$ quit
```

Then, run the Pig script as follows:

```
$  pig hdfs-to-hbase.pig
```

Now watch the console output. Pig will execute the script as a MapReduce job. Even though we are only importing two small files here, we can insert a fairly large amount of data by exploiting the parallelism of MapReduce.

At the end of the run, Pig will print out some statistics:

```
Input(s):
Successfully read 7 records (591 bytes) from: "hdfs://quickstart.
cloudera:8020/user/cloudera/hbase-import"
Output(s):
Successfully stored 7 records in: "hbase://sensors"
```

Looks good! We should have seven rows in our HBase `sensors` table. We can inspect the table from the HBase shell with the following commands:

```
$ hbase shell
$ scan 'sensors'
```

This is how your output might look:

```
ROW                         COLUMN+CELL
 sensor11                   column=f:max, timestamp=1412373703149,
value=90
 sensor11                   column=f:min, timestamp=1412373703149,
value=70
 sensor22                   column=f:max, timestamp=1412373703177,
value=80
 sensor22                   column=f:min, timestamp=1412373703177,
value=70
```

```
 sensor31                   column=f:max, timestamp=1412373703177,
value=85

 sensor31                   column=f:min, timestamp=1412373703177,
value=72

 sensor33                   column=f:max, timestamp=1412373703177,
value=75

 sensor33                   column=f:min, timestamp=1412373703177,
value=72

 sensor44                   column=f:max, timestamp=1412373703184,
value=55

 sensor44                   column=f:min, timestamp=1412373703184,
value=42

 sensor45                   column=f:max, timestamp=1412373703184,
value=57

 sensor45                   column=f:min, timestamp=1412373703184,
value=47

 sensor55                   column=f:max, timestamp=1412373703184,
value=55

 sensor55                   column=f:min, timestamp=1412373703184,
value=42

7 row(s) in 0.0820 seconds
```

There you go; you can see that seven rows have been inserted!

With Pig, it was very easy. It took us just two lines of Pig script to do the import.

Java MapReduce

We have just demonstrated MapReduce using Pig, and you now know that Pig is a concise and high-level way to write MapReduce programs. This is demonstrated by our previous script, essentially the two lines of Pig code. However, there are situations where you do want to use the Java API, and it would make more sense to use it than using a Pig script. This can happen when you need Java to access Java libraries or do some other detailed tasks for which Pig is not a good match. For that, we have provided the Java version of the MapReduce code in our GitHub repository.

Using HBase's bulk loader utility

HBase is shipped with a bulk loader tool called **ImportTsv** that can import files from HDFS into HBase tables directly. It is very easy to use, and as a bonus, it uses MapReduce internally to process files in parallel.

Perform the following steps to use ImportTsv:

1. Stage data files into HDFS (remember that the files are processed using MapReduce).
2. Create a table in HBase if required.
3. Run the import.

Staging data files into HDFS

The first step to stage data files into HDFS has already been outlined in the previous section. The following sections explain the next two steps to stage data files.

Creating an HBase table

We will do this from the HBase shell. A note on regions is in order here. Regions are shards created automatically by HBase. It is the regions that are responsible for the distributed nature of HBase. However, you need to pay some attention to them in order to assure performance. If you put all the data in one region, you will cause what is called region hotspotting, as we mentioned in *Chapter 5, Time Series Data*.

What is especially nice about a bulk loader is that when creating a table, it lets you presplit the table into multiple regions.

Precreating regions will allow faster imports (because the insert requests will go out to multiple region servers).

Here, we are creating a single column family:

```
$  hbase shell
hbase> create 'sensors', {NAME => 'f'},  {SPLITS => ['sensor20',
'sensor40', 'sensor60']}
0 row(s) in 1.3940 seconds
=> Hbase::Table - sensors


hbase > describe 'sensors'
DESCRIPTION                                          ENABLED
```

```
'sensors', {NAME => 'f', DATA_BLOCK_ENCODING =>   true
'NONE', BLOOMFILTER => 'ROW', REPLICATION_SCOPE
=> '0', VERSIONS => '1', COMPRESSION => 'NONE',
MIN_VERSIONS => '0', TTL => 'FOREVER', KEEP_DELE
TED_CELLS => 'false', BLOCKSIZE => '65536', IN_M
EMORY => 'false', BLOCKCACHE => 'true'}
1 row(s) in 0.1140 seconds
```

We are creating regions here. Why there are exactly four regions will be clear from the following diagram:

Table Regions

Name	Region Server	Start Key	End Key	Requests
sensors,,1409085502023.2406c522c2c7d594b87358cc75a7a159.	localhost:60020		sensor20	0
sensors,sensor20,1409085502023.98724018a71748d77095e2ee166d0315.	localhost:60020	sensor20	sensor40	0
sensors,sensor40,1409085502023.6f9a38b0d4eeb0d9395c1bdc26690b79.	localhost:60020	sensor40	sensor60	0
sensors,sensor60,1409085502023.22db462b5736b3291add2733f34a9f4d.	localhost:60020	sensor60		0

On inspecting the table in the HBase Master UI, we will see this. Also, you can see how **Start Key** and **End Key**, which we specified, are showing up.

Run the import

Ok, now it's time to insert data into HBase.

To see the usage of ImportTsv, do the following:

```
$ hbase  org.apache.hadoop.hbase.mapreduce.ImportTsv
```

This will print the usage as follows:

```
$ hbase  org.apache.hadoop.hbase.mapreduce.ImportTsv \
-Dimporttsv.separator=,  \
-Dimporttsv.columns=HBASE_ROW_KEY,f:max,f:min \
sensors  hbase-import/
```

The following table explains what the parameters mean:

Parameter	Description
`-Dimporttsv.separator`	Here, our separator is a comma (,).
	The default value is tab (\t).
`-Dimporttsv.columns=HBASE_ROW_KEY,f:max,f:min \`	This is where we map our input files into HBase tables.
	The first field, `sensor_id`, is our key, and we use `HBASE_ROW_KEY` to denote that the rest we are inserting into column family `f`.
	The second field, `max temp`, maps to `f:max`.
	The last field, `min temp`, maps to `f:min`.
`sensors`	This is the table name.
`hbase-import`	This is the HDFS directory where the data files are located.

When we run this command, we will see that a MapReduce job is being kicked off. This is how an import is parallelized.

Also, from the console output, we can see that MapReduce is importing two files as follows:

```
[main] mapreduce.JobSubmitter: number of splits:2
```

While the job is running, we can inspect the progress from YARN (or the JobTracker UI).

One thing that we can note is that the MapReduce job only consists of mappers. This is because we are reading a bunch of files and inserting them into HBase directly. There is nothing to aggregate. So, there is no need for reducers.

After the job is done, inspect the counters and we can see this:

```
Map-Reduce Framework
  Map input records=7
  Map output records=7
```

This tells us that mappers read seven records from the files and inserted seven records into HBase.

Let's also verify the data in HBase:

```
$   hbase   shell
hbase >   scan 'sensors'
```

```
ROW                      COLUMN+CELL
 sensor11                column=f:max, timestamp=1409087465345, value=90
 sensor11                column=f:min, timestamp=1409087465345, value=70
 sensor22                column=f:max, timestamp=1409087465345, value=80
 sensor22                column=f:min, timestamp=1409087465345, value=70
 sensor31                column=f:max, timestamp=1409087465345, value=85
 sensor31                column=f:min, timestamp=1409087465345, value=72
 sensor33                column=f:max, timestamp=1409087465345, value=75
 sensor33                column=f:min, timestamp=1409087465345, value=72
 sensor44                column=f:max, timestamp=1409087465345, value=55
 sensor44                column=f:min, timestamp=1409087465345, value=42
 sensor45                column=f:max, timestamp=1409087465345, value=57
 sensor45                column=f:min, timestamp=1409087465345, value=47
 sensor55                column=f:max, timestamp=1409087465345, value=55
 sensor55                column=f:min, timestamp=1409087465345, value=42
7 row(s) in 2.1180 seconds
```

Your output might vary slightly.

We can see that seven rows are inserted, confirming the MapReduce counters!

Let's take another quick look at the HBase UI, which is shown here:

Table Regions

Name	Region Server	Start Key	End Key	Requests
sensors,,1409085502023.2406c522c2c7d594b87358cc75a7a159.	localhost:60020		sensor20	2
sensors,sensor20,1409085502023.98724018a71748d77095e2ee166d0315.	localhost:60020	sensor20	sensor40	4
sensors,sensor40,1409085502023.6f9a38b0d4eeb0d9395c1bdc26690b79.	localhost:60020	sensor40	sensor60	4
sensors,sensor60,1409085502023.22db462b5736b3291add2733f34a9f4d.	localhost:60020	sensor60		0

As you can see, the inserts go to different regions. So, on a HBase cluster with many region servers, the load will be spread across the cluster. This is because we have presplit the table into regions. Here are some questions to test your understanding.

Run the same ImportTsv command again and see how many records are in the table. Do you get duplicates? Try to find the answer and explain why that is the correct answer, then check these in the book's GitHub repository.

Bulk import scenarios

Here are a few bulk import scenarios:

Scenario	Methods	Notes
The data is already in HDFS and needs to be imported into HBase.	The two methods that can be used to do this are as follows: • If the ImportTsv tool can work for you, then use it as it will save time in writing custom MapReduce code. • Sometimes, you might have to write a custom MapReduce job to import (for example, complex time series data, doing data mapping, and so on).	It is probably a good idea to presplit the table before a bulk import. This spreads the insert requests across the cluster and results in a higher insert rate. If you are writing a custom MapReduce job, consider using a high-level MapReduce platform such as Pig or Hive. They are much more concise to write than the Java code.
The data is in another database (RDBMs/NoSQL) and you need to import it into HBase.	Use a utility such as **Sqoop** to bring the data into HDFS and then use the tools outlined in the first scenario.	Avoid writing MapReduce code that directly queries databases. Most databases cannot handle many simultaneous connections. It is best to bring the data into Hadoop (HDFS) first and then use MapReduce.

Profiling HBase applications

Just like any software development process, once we have our HBase application working correctly, we would want to make it faster. At times, developers get too carried away and start optimizing before the application is finalized. There is a well-known rule that premature optimization is the root of all evil. One of the sources for this rule is Scott Meyers *Effective C++*.

We can perform some ad hoc profiling in our code by timing various function calls. Also, we can use profiling tools to pinpoint the trouble spots. Using profiling tools is highly encouraged for the following reasons:

- Profiling takes out the guesswork (and a good majority of developers' guesses are wrong).

- There is no need to modify the code. Manual profiling means that we have to go and insert the instrumentation code all over the code. Profilers work by inspecting the runtime behavior.

- Most profilers have a nice and intuitive UI to visualize the program flow and time flow.

The authors use **JProfiler**. It is a pretty effective profiler. However, it is neither free nor open source. So, for the purpose of this chapter, we are going to show you a simple manual profiling, as follows:

```
public class UserInsert {

    static String tableName = "users";
    static String familyName = "info";

    public static void main(String[] args) throws Exception {
        Configuration config = HBaseConfiguration.create();
        // change the following to connect to remote clusters
        // config.set("hbase.zookeeper.quorum", "localhost");
        long t1a = System.currentTimeMillis();
        HTable htable = new HTable(config, tableName);
        long t1b = System.currentTimeMillis();
        System.out.println ("Connected to HTable in : " +
(t1b-t1a) + " ms");
        int total = 100;
        long t2a = System.currentTimeMillis();
        for (int i = 0; i < total; i++) {
            int userid = i;
            String email = "user-" + i + "@foo.com";
```

```
            String phone = "555-1234";

            byte[] key = Bytes.toBytes(userid);
            Put put = new Put(key);

            put.add(Bytes.toBytes(familyName),
Bytes.toBytes("email"), Bytes.toBytes(email));
            put.add(Bytes.toBytes(familyName),
Bytes.toBytes("phone"), Bytes.toBytes(phone));
            htable.put(put);

        }
        long t2b = System.currentTimeMillis();
        System.out.println("inserted " + total + " users  in " +
(t2b - t2a) + " ms");
        htable.close();

    }
}
```

The code we just saw inserts some sample user data into HBase. We are profiling two operations, that is, connection time and actual insert time.

A sample run of the Java application yields the following:

```
Connected to HTable in : 1139 ms
inserted 100 users  in 350 ms
```

We spent a lot of time in connecting to HBase. This makes sense. The connection process has to go to ZooKeeper first and then to HBase. So, it is an expensive operation. How can we minimize the connection cost?

The answer is by using connection pooling. Luckily, for us, HBase comes with a connection pool manager. The Java class for this is HConnectionManager. It is very simple to use.

Let's update our class to use HConnectionManager:

```
Code : File name: hbase_dp.ch8.UserInsert2.java

package hbase_dp.ch8;
```

```
import org.apache.hadoop.conf.Configuration;
import org.apache.hadoop.hbase.HBaseConfiguration;
import org.apache.hadoop.hbase.client.HConnection;
import org.apache.hadoop.hbase.client.HConnectionManager;
import org.apache.hadoop.hbase.client.HTable;
import org.apache.hadoop.hbase.client.HTableInterface;
import org.apache.hadoop.hbase.client.Put;
import org.apache.hadoop.hbase.util.Bytes;

public class UserInsert2 {

    static String tableName = "users";
     static String familyName = "info";

    public static void main(String[] args) throws Exception {
        Configuration config = HBaseConfiguration.create();
        // change the following to connect to remote clusters
        // config.set("hbase.zookeeper.quorum", "localhost");

        long t1a = System.currentTimeMillis();
        HConnection hConnection = HConnectionManager.
createConnection(config);
        long t1b = System.currentTimeMillis();
        System.out.println ("Connection manager in : " +
(t1b-t1a) + " ms");

        // simulate the first 'connection'
        long t2a = System.currentTimeMillis();
        HTableInterface htable = hConnection.getTable(tableName) ;
        long t2b = System.currentTimeMillis();
        System.out.println ("first connection in : " + (t2b-t2a) +
" ms");

        // second connection
        long t3a = System.currentTimeMillis();
        HTableInterface htable2 = hConnection.getTable(tableName)
;
        long t3b = System.currentTimeMillis();
        System.out.println ("second connection : " + (t3b-t3a) +
" ms");

        int total = 100;
        long t4a = System.currentTimeMillis();
```

```
        for (int i = 0; i < total; i++) {
            int userid = i;
            String email = "user-" + i + "@foo.com";
            String phone = "555-1234";

            byte[] key = Bytes.toBytes(userid);
            Put put = new Put(key);

            put.add(Bytes.toBytes(familyName), Bytes.toBytes("email"),
Bytes.toBytes(email));
            put.add(Bytes.toBytes(familyName), Bytes.toBytes("phone"),
Bytes.toBytes(phone));
            htable.put(put);

        }
        long t4b = System.currentTimeMillis();
        System.out.println("inserted " + total + " users  in " +
(t4b - t4a) + " ms");

        hConnection.close();
    }
}
```

A sample run yields the following timings:

```
Connection manager in : 98 ms
first connection in : 808 ms
second connection : 0 ms
inserted 100 users  in 393 ms
```

The first connection takes a long time, but then take a look at the time of the second connection. It is almost instant ! This is cool!

> If you are connecting to HBase from web applications (or interactive applications), use connection pooling.

More tips for high-performing HBase writes

Here we will discuss some techniques and best practices to improve writes in HBase.

Batch writes

Currently, in our code, each time we call `htable.put (one_put)`, we make an RPC call to an HBase region server. This round-trip delay can be minimized if we call `htable.put()` with a bunch of put records. Then, with one round trip, we can insert a bunch of records into HBase. This is called **batch puts**.

Here is an example of batch puts. Only the relevant section is shown for clarity. For the full code, see `hbase_dp.ch8.UserInsert3.java`:

```
int total = 100;
long t4a = System.currentTimeMillis();
List<Put> puts = new ArrayList<>();
for (int i = 0; i < total; i++) {
    int userid = i;
    String email = "user-" + i + "@foo.com";
    String phone = "555-1234";

    byte[] key = Bytes.toBytes(userid);
    Put put = new Put(key);

    put.add(Bytes.toBytes(familyName), Bytes.toBytes("email"),
Bytes.toBytes(email));
    put.add(Bytes.toBytes(familyName), Bytes.toBytes("phone"),
Bytes.toBytes(phone));

    puts.add(put); // just add to the list
}
htable.put(puts);  // do a batch put
long t4b = System.currentTimeMillis();
System.out.println("inserted " + total + " users  in " + (t4b
- t4a) + " ms");
```

A sample run with a batch put is as follows:

```
inserted 100 users  in 48 ms
```

The same code with individual puts took around 350 milliseconds!

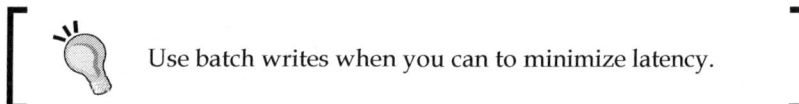

> Use batch writes when you can to minimize latency.

Note that the `HTableUtil` class that comes with HBase implements some smart batching options for your use and enjoyment.

Setting memory buffers

We can control when the puts are flushed by setting the `client write buffer` option. Once the data in the memory exceeds this setting, it is flushed to disk. The default setting is `2 M`. Its purpose is to limit how much data is stored in the buffer before writing it to disk.

There are two ways of setting this:

- In `hbase-site.xml` (this setting will be cluster-wide):

```
<property>
  <name>hbase.client.write.buffer</name>
  <value>8388608</value>   <!-- 8 M -->
</property>
```

- In the application (only applies for that application):

```
htable.setWriteBufferSize(1024*1024*10); // 10
```

Keep in mind that a bigger buffer takes more memory on both the client side and the server side. As a practical guideline, estimate how much memory you can dedicate to the client and put the rest of the load on the cluster.

Turning off autofush

If **autoflush** is enabled, each `htable.put()` object incurs a round trip RPC call to `HRegionServer`. Turning autoflush off can reduce the number of round trips and decrease latency. To turn it off, use this code:

```
htable.setAutoFlush(false);
```

The risk of turning off autoflush is if the client crashes before the data is sent to HBase, it will result in a data loss. Still, when will you want to do it? The answer is: when the danger of data loss is not important and speed is paramount. Also, see the batch write recommendations we saw previously.

Turning off WAL

Before we discuss this, we need to emphasize that the **write-ahead log (WAL)** is there to prevent data loss in the case of server crashes. By turning it off, we are bypassing this protection. Be very careful when choosing this. Bulk loading is one of the cases where turning off WAL might make sense.

To turn off WAL, set it for each put:

```
put.setDurability(Durability.SKIP_WAL);
```

More tips for high-performing HBase reads

So far, we looked at tips to write data into HBase. Now, let's take a look at some tips to read data faster.

The scan cache

When reading a large number of rows, it is better to set scan caching to a high number (in the 100 seconds or 1,000 seconds range). Otherwise, each row that is scanned will result in a trip to `HRegionServer`. This is especially encouraged for MapReduce jobs as they will likely consume a lot of rows sequentially.

To set scan caching, use the following code:

```
Scan scan = new Scan();
scan.setCaching(1000);
```

Only read the families or columns needed

When fetching a row, by default, HBase returns all the families and all the columns. If you only care about one family or a few attributes, specifying them will save needless I/O.

To specify a family, use this:

```
scan.addFamily( Bytes.toBytes("familiy1"));
```

To specify columns, use this:

```
scan.addColumn( Bytes.toBytes("familiy1"),
Bytes.toBytes("col1"))
```

The block cache

When scanning large rows sequentially (say in MapReduce), it is recommended that you turn off the block cache. Turning off the cache might be completely counter-intuitive. However, caches are only effective when we repeatedly access the same rows. During sequential scanning, there is no caching, and turning on the block cache will introduce a lot of churning in the cache (new data is constantly brought into the cache and old data is evicted to make room for the new data).

So, we have the following points to consider:

- Turn off the block cache for sequential scans
- Turn off the block cache for random/repeated access

Benchmarking or load testing HBase

Benchmarking is a good way to verify HBase's setup and performance. There are a few good benchmarks available:

- HBase's built-in benchmark
- The **Yahoo Cloud Serving Benchmark (YCSB)**
- **JMeter** for custom workloads

HBase's built-in benchmark

HBase's built-in benchmark is PerformanceEvaluation.

To find its usage, use this:

```
$   hbase   org.apache.hadoop.hbase.PerformanceEvaluation
```

To perform a write benchmark, use this:

```
$ hbase  org.apache.hadoop.hbase.PerformanceEvaluation   --nomapred
randomWrite 5
```

Here we are using five threads and no MapReduce.

To accurately measure the throughput, we need to presplit the table that the benchmark writes to. It is `TestTable`.

```
$ hbase  org.apache.hadoop.hbase.PerformanceEvaluation   --nomapred
--presplit=3   randomWrite 5
```

Here, the table is split in three ways. It is good practice to split the table into as many regions as the number of region servers.

There is a read option along with a whole host of scan options.

YCSB

The YCSB is a comprehensive benchmark suite that works with many systems such as Cassandra, Accumulo, and HBase.

Download it from GitHub, as follows:

```
$    git clone git://github.com/brianfrankcooper/YCSB.git
```

Build it like this:

```
$ mvn -DskipTests package
```

Create an HBase table to test against:

```
$  hbase shell
hbase> create 'ycsb', 'f1'
```

Now, copy `hdfs-site.xml` for your cluster into the `hbase/src/main/conf/` directory and run the benchmark:

```
$  bin/ycsb load hbase -P workloads/workloada -p columnfamily=f1 -p
table=ycsb
```

> YCSB offers lots of workloads and options. Please refer to its wiki page at `https://github.com/brianfrankcooper/YCSB/wiki`.

JMeter for custom workloads

The standard benchmarks will give you an idea of your HBase cluster's performance. However, nothing can substitute measuring your own workload.

We want to measure at least the insert speed or the query speed.

We also want to run a stress test. So, we can measure the ceiling on how much our HBase cluster can support.

We can do a simple instrumentation as we did earlier too. However, there are tools such as JMeter that can help us with load testing.

Setting up using JMeter is beyond the scope of this book. Please refer to the JMeter website and check out the Hadoop or HBase plugins for JMeter.

Monitoring HBase

Running any distributed system involves decent monitoring. HBase is no exception. Luckily, HBase has the following capabilities:

- HBase exposes a lot of metrics
- These metrics can be directly consumed by monitoring systems such as Ganglia
- We can also obtain these metrics in the JSON format via the REST interface and JMX

Monitoring is a big subject and we consider it as part HBase administration. So, in this section, we will give pointers to tools and utilities that allow you to monitor HBase.

Ganglia

Ganglia is a generic system monitor that can monitor hosts (such as CPU, disk usage, and so on). The Hadoop stack has had a pretty good integration with Ganglia for some time now. HBase and Ganglia integration is set up by modern installers from Cloudera and Hortonworks.

To enable Ganglia metrics, update the `hadoop-metrics.properties` file in the HBase configuration directory. Here's a sample file:

```
hbase.class=org.apache.hadoop.metrics.ganglia.GangliaContext31
hbase.period=10
hbase.servers=ganglia-server:PORT
jvm.class=org.apache.hadoop.metrics.ganglia.GangliaContext31
jvm.period=10
jvm.servers=ganglia-server:PORT
rpc.class=org.apache.hadoop.metrics.ganglia.GangliaContext31
rpc.period=10
rpc.servers=ganglia-server:PORT
```

This file has to be uploaded to all the HBase servers (master servers as well as region servers).

Here are some sample graphs from Ganglia (these are Wikimedia statistics, for example):

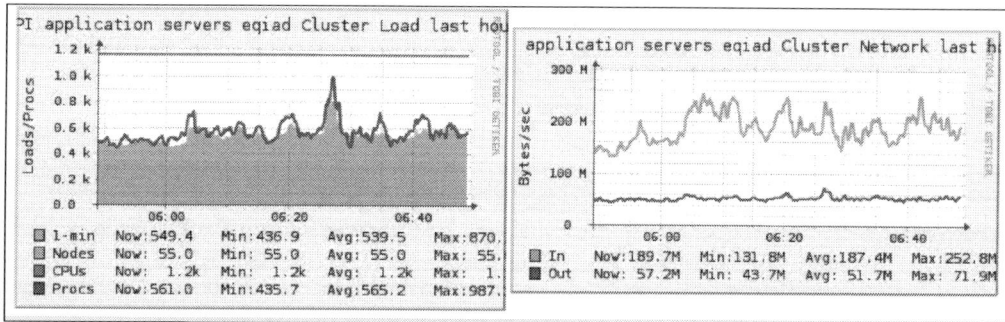

These graphs show cluster-wide resource utilization.

OpenTSDB

OpenTSDB is a scalable time series database, which we mentioned in *Chapter 5, Time Series Data*. It can collect and visualize metrics on a large scale. OpenTSDB uses **collectors**, light-weight agents that send metrics to the open TSDB server to collect metrics, and there is a collector library that can collect metrics from HBase.

> You can see all the collectors at `http://opentsdb.net/docs/build/html/user_guide/utilities/tcollector.html`.

An interesting factoid is that OpenTSDB is built on Hadoop/HBase.

Collecting metrics via the JMX interface

HBase exposes a lot of metrics via JMX.

This page can be accessed from the web dashboard at `http://<hbase master>:60010/jmx`.

For example, for a HBase instance that is running locally, it will be `http://localhost:60010/jmx`.

Here is a sample screenshot of the JMX metrics via the web UI:

```
←  →  X   □ 192.168.1.126:60010/jmx

{
  - beans: [
    - {
          name: "java.lang:type=Memory",
          modelerType: "sun.management.MemoryImpl",
        - HeapMemoryUsage: {
              committed: 60751872,
              init: 62765632,
              max: 1039859712,
              used: 19610000
          },
        - NonHeapMemoryUsage: {
              committed: 41222144,
              init: 24313856,
              max: 136314880,
              used: 40552400
          },
          ObjectPendingFinalizationCount: 0,
          Verbose: false,
          ObjectName: "java.lang:type=Memory"
      },
```

Here's a quick example of how to programmatically retrieve these metrics using `curl`:

```
$  curl  'localhost:60010/jmx'
```

Since this is a web service, we can write a script/application in any language (Java, Python, or Ruby) to retrieve and inspect the metrics.

Summary

In this chapter, you learned how to push the performance of our HBase applications up. We looked at how to effectively load a large amount of data into HBase. You also learned about benchmarking and monitoring HBase and saw tips on how to do high-performing reads/writes.

With this, we conclude the book. We hope it's been a fun journey for you. Please visit the book's site, http://hbasedesignpatterns.com, and on the GitHub repository, https://github.com/elephantscale/hbase-book. While the book itself cannot be updated (even though some books can; you can check here: http://bit.ly/1Ec1V7H), we plan to keep the repository updated with fixes and more examples.

Index

J

Java MapReduce 111
JMeter 124, 125
JProfiler 117

K

KairosDB
  URL 77
Kiji
  about 35
  URL 6

L

larger binary files, handling
  Amazon S3 storage 60
  approaches 58
  Facebook's Haystack 59
  Google Blobstore 58
  multistep approach 61
  practical approach 60
  practical lab 61
  Twitter solution 59
lists 50
lookup tables 83

M

Mac 15
many-to-many relationship
  about 92
  applying, for video site 97, 98
  creating, for social network 95-97
  creating, for university with students
      and courses 92-95
MapR 28
MapReduce
  about 107
  used, for importing data into HBase 107
maps 50
memory buffers
  setting 122
metrics
  collecting, via JMX interface 127, 128

MongoDB

MongoDB
  URL 40
multistep approach, for storing larger
    files 61

N

NoSQL 6, 29

O

objects
  storing, for user 81, 82
Open Software Foundation (OSF) 56
OpenTSDB
  about 73, 127
  architecture 74
  compactions 76
  overall design 75
  URL, for design documentation 77
  row key 75
  timestamp 76
  tools, using 74, 75
  UID table schema 77

P

passwords
  lost passwords, dealing with 82, 83
PerformanceEvaluation 124
performance optimization, HBase
  about 105
  bulk data, loading 105-107
  data, importing from HDFS 108, 109
  data, importing with MapReduce 107
  HBase applications, profiling 117-120
  HBase, benchmarking 124
  HBase, load testing 124
  HBase, monitoring 126
performance testing
  data, generating for 84-87
Phoenix
  about 39, 40
  installing 40-43
  URL 39
Pig 109
popularity contest
  counters used 87, 88

W

write-ahead log (WAL)
enabling 122
WibiData 35

Y

Yahoo Cloud Serving Benchmark (YCSB)
about 124, 125
URL 125

Z

ZooKeeper
URL 59

[PACKT] PUBLISHING | open source *
community experience distilled

Thank you for buying
HBase Design Patterns

About Packt Publishing

Packt, pronounced 'packed', published its first book, *Mastering phpMyAdmin for Effective MySQL Management*, in April 2004, and subsequently continued to specialize in publishing highly focused books on specific technologies and solutions.

Our books and publications share the experiences of your fellow IT professionals in adapting and customizing today's systems, applications, and frameworks. Our solution-based books give you the knowledge and power to customize the software and technologies you're using to get the job done. Packt books are more specific and less general than the IT books you have seen in the past. Our unique business model allows us to bring you more focused information, giving you more of what you need to know, and less of what you don't.

Packt is a modern yet unique publishing company that focuses on producing quality, cutting-edge books for communities of developers, administrators, and newbies alike. For more information, please visit our website at www.packtpub.com.

About Packt Open Source

In 2010, Packt launched two new brands, Packt Open Source and Packt Enterprise, in order to continue its focus on specialization. This book is part of the Packt Open Source brand, home to books published on software built around open source licenses, and offering information to anybody from advanced developers to budding web designers. The Open Source brand also runs Packt's Open Source Royalty Scheme, by which Packt gives a royalty to each open source project about whose software a book is sold.

Writing for Packt

We welcome all inquiries from people who are interested in authoring. Book proposals should be sent to author@packtpub.com. If your book idea is still at an early stage and you would like to discuss it first before writing a formal book proposal, then please contact us; one of our commissioning editors will get in touch with you.

We're not just looking for published authors; if you have strong technical skills but no writing experience, our experienced editors can help you develop a writing career, or simply get some additional reward for your expertise.

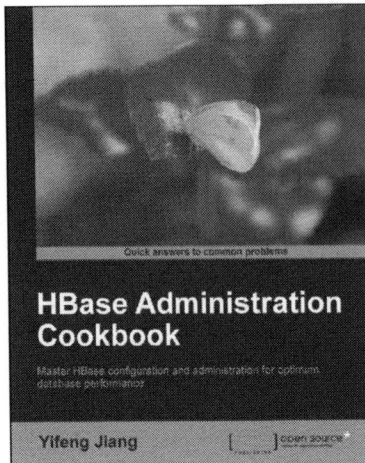

HBase Administration Cookbook

ISBN: 978-1-84951-714-0   Paperback: 332 pages

Master HBase configuration and administration for optimum database performance

1. Move large amounts of data into HBase and learn how to manage it efficiently.

2. Set up HBase on the cloud, get it ready for production, and run it smoothly with high performance.

3. Maximize the ability of HBase with the Hadoop eco-system including HDFS, MapReduce, Zookeeper, and Hive.

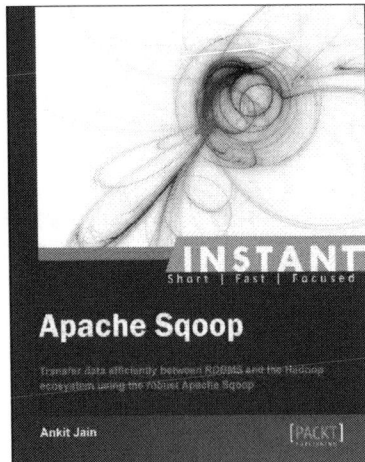

Instant Apache Sqoop

ISBN: 978-1-78216-576-7   Paperback: 58 pages

Transfer data efficiently between RDBMS and the Hadoop ecosystem using the robust Apache Sqoop

1. Learn something new in an Instant! A short, fast, focused guide delivering immediate results.

2. Learn how to transfer data between RDBMS and Hadoop using Sqoop.

3. Add a third-party connector into Sqoop.

4. Export data from Hadoop and Hive to RDBMS.

Please check **www.PacktPub.com** for information on our titles

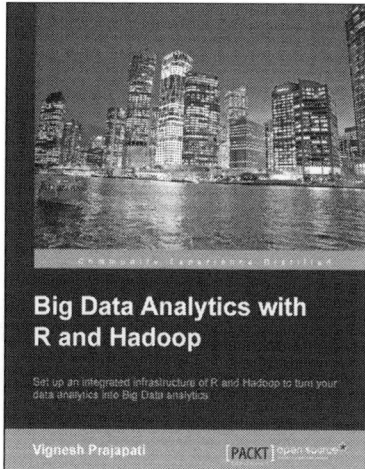

Big Data Analytics with R and Hadoop

ISBN: 978-1-78216-328-2   Paperback: 238 pages

Set up an integrated infrastructure of R and Hadoop to turn your data analytics into Big Data analytics

1. Write Hadoop MapReduce within R.

2. Learn data analytics with R and the Hadoop platform.

3. Handle HDFS data within R.

4. Understand Hadoop streaming with R.

5. Encode and enrich datasets into R.

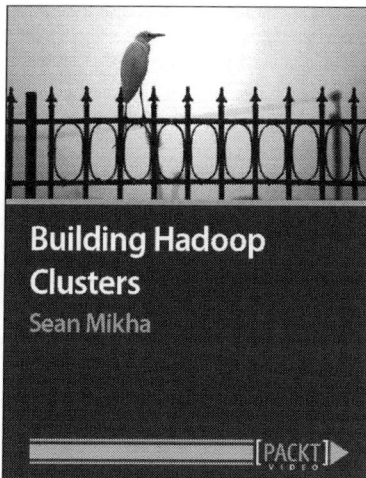

Building Hadoop Clusters [Video]

ISBN: 978-1-78328-403-0   Duration: 02:34 hours

Deploy multi-node Hadoop clusters to harness the Cloud for storage and large-scale data processing

1. Familiarize yourself with Hadoop and its services, and how to configure them.

2. Deploy compute instances and set up a three-node Hadoop cluster on Amazon.

3. Set up a Linux installation optimized for Hadoop.

Please check **www.PacktPub.com** for information on our titles

Printed in Great Britain
by Amazon.co.uk, Ltd.,
Marston Gate.